Innovation in Risk Analysis

Series Editor

Jianping Li, School of Economics and Management, University of Chinese Academy of Science, Beijing, China

This book series focuses on discussing the new theories, new models, and new methods of risk analysis. Moreover, the better risk management practices in the areas of social, physical and health sciences, engineering, public policy and administration, and media and communication studies will priority attention.

The book series aims to publish the latest theoretical and empirical research on the communication, regulation, and management of risk. Research that you might want to contribute to the book series could explore:

- The Inter-relationships between risk, decision-making and society.
- How to promote better risk management practices.
- Contribute to the development of risk management methodologies in the different areas.

Jue Liu

Risk Management in Public Health

Springer

Jue Liu
School of Public Health
Peking University
Beijing, China

ISSN 2731-6254 ISSN 2731-6262 (electronic)
Innovation in Risk Analysis
ISBN 978-981-97-6825-7 ISBN 978-981-97-6826-4 (eBook)
https://doi.org/10.1007/978-981-97-6826-4

This Springer imprint is published by the registered company Springer Nature Singapore Pte Ltd.
The registered company address is: 152 Beach Road, #21-01/04 Gateway East, Singapore 189721, Singapore

Editorial Committee

Editor-in-Chief:

Editorial Board Members:

Publisher:

Springer

Preface

Public health risk management is an interdisciplinary science that involves a number of fields, including epidemiology, statistics, public policy and social science. With the acceleration of globalization, environmental changes and increased mobility of populations, the risks of public health have become increasingly complex and diverse. In recent years, global epidemics of emerging infectious diseases, such as COVID-19 and mpox, as well as the continuing threat of other infectious diseases, such as malaria and viral hepatitis, have further emphasized the importance of effective public health risk management.

In modern society, public health risk management is not only the responsibility of governments and health organizations, but also a task shared by society as a whole. Globalization has accelerated the spread of diseases, and health problems in a single country or region may rapidly evolve into a global health crisis. Therefore, international cooperation and information sharing have become particularly critical in public health risk management. The World Health Organization (WHO) and national governments play an indispensable role in responding to emerging and re-emerging infectious diseases and in developing public health strategies and contingency plans. In addition, public health risk management is not only about responding to emergencies, but also about managing long-standing health threats. It requires us to strengthen the construction of disease surveillance, risk assessment and early warning systems in our daily work, and to improve our capacity of early detection and rapid response to diseases. It is also required to develop and improve public health policies and regulations to ensure that risk management is scientific and standardized.

Advances in science and technology have greatly promoted the innovative development and practice of public health risk management. Taking advantage of the theoretical background and practical research experience in the field of public health risk management, the editor-in-chief of this book has organized a group of young experts, combined with domestic and international research advances, to write *Risk Management in Public Health*, aiming to provide a systematic framework for public health risk management, and to provide readers with a comprehensive demonstration, from theory to practice, of how to effectively identify, analyze, assess and respond to various public health risks.

The book is divided into two parts. Part I is "*Theories of Risk Management in Public Health*", which covers the basic concepts of public health risk, theories and approaches of risk assessment, surveillance and early warning systems, as well as theories and approaches of risk assessment of infectious diseases, public health emergency management, risk management and decision-making. Part II is "*Practices of Risk Management in Public Health*", which takes major infectious diseases in the world for example, such as COVID-19, mpox, malaria and viral hepatitis, and describes in detail specific cases of risk management practices in terms of disease burden, risk assessment, surveillance and early-warning, prevention and control strategies, and effect evaluation.

Through a systematic theoretical introduction and detailed practical examples, we hope to help readers fully understand and master the basic theories, methods and practical applications of public health risk management. Whether you are a public health professional, a policymaker or a researcher, we hope that this book can be a bright light for you in the field of public health risk management, and lead you to move forward on the road of promoting public health. We also extend our gratitude to the National Natural Science Foundation of China (Grant No. 72122001) for their support, which has made this work possible.

Beijing, China Jue Liu
May 2024

Contents

Abbreviations

AFP	Acute flaccid paralysis
Ag	Antigen
AHP	Analytic hierarchy process
AIDS	Acquired immunodeficiency syndrome
ALT	Alanine aminotransferase
anti-HAV	Antibody against hepatitis A virus
anti-HBc	Antibody against hepatitis B core antigen
anti-HCV	Antibody against hepatitis C virus
anti-HEV	Antibody against hepatitis E virus
AWD	Acute watery diarrhea
BRFSS	Behavior risk factors surveillance system
CDC	Centers for diseases control and prevention
COVID-19	Coronavirus disease 2019
DHIS2	District health information software version 2
DR Congo	Democratic Republic of the Congo
ECDC	European center for disease prevention and control
eDEWS	Electronic disease early warning system
EDM	Emergency decision-making
EOC	Emergency operations center
ERF	Emergency response framework
EWAR	Early warning alert and response
EWRS	European early warning and response system
FPT	Federal/provincial/territorial
GDP	Gross domestic product
GIS	Geographic information system
GTS	Global technical strategy for malaria 2016 – 2030
HAV	Hepatitis A virus
HBsAg	Hepatitis B surface antigen
HBV	Hepatitis B virus
HCC	Hepatocellular carcinoma
HCV	Hepatitis C virus

HDV	Hepatitis D virus
HEV	Hepatitis E virus
HIV	Human immunodeficiency virus
IAR	Infected averted ratio
ICER	Incremental cost-effectiveness ratio
Ig	Immunoglobulin
IHR	International health regulations
ILI	Influenza-like illness
IMS	Incident management system
IPTp	Intermittent preventive treatment for pregnant women
IPTsc	Intermittent preventive treatment for school-aged children
IRS	Indoor residual spraying
IRV	Infectivity - receptivity – vulnerability
ISO	The international organization for standardization
ITNs	Insecticide-treated nets
MDA	Mass drug administrations
MDR-TB	Multidrug-resistant TB
MERS	Middle east respiratory syndrome
MONICA	Monitoring of trends and determinants in cardiovascular disease
MSM	Men who make sex with men
NCI	National cancer institute
NHS	National health service
NRC	National research council
PDMC	Post-discharge malaria chemoprevention
PHEIC	Public health emergency of international concern
PHEMLS	Public health emergency management legal system
PMC	Perennial malaria chemoprevention
RNA	Ribonucleic acid
RR-TB	Rifampicin-resistant TB
SARS	Severe acute respiratory syndrome
SDGs	Sustainable development goals
SEIR	Susceptible exposed infected recovered
SI	Susceptible infected
SIR	Susceptible infected recovered
SIRS	Susceptible infected recovered susceptible
SMC	Seasonal malaria chemoprevention
STD	Sexually transmitted disease
TB	Tuberculosis
UHC	Universal health coverage
UI	Uncertain interval
UN	United nations
WHO	World health organization

List of Figures

List of Tables

Part I
Theories of Risk Management in Public Health

Chapter 1
Overview of Public Health Risk

1.1 Definition and Characteristics of Public Health

1.1.1 Definition of Public Health

Public health can be understood as an organized social endeavor that requires the combined efforts of multiple disciplines. It may also be seen as a form of technology and practical activity. The purpose and core of public health are the health of the populace. With the progress of the times and scientific advancements, our understanding of public health continually deepens. Authorities and academics across diverse disciplines have elucidated the significance and distinctiveness of the societal endeavor pertaining to public health from manifold perspectives.

In 1920, Charles-Edward A. Winslow, the leading figure in American public health, described public health as "*Public health is the science and art of preventing disease, prolonging life, and promoting health through the organized efforts and informed choices of society, organizations, public and private, communities and individuals.*" This definition, adopted by the World Health Organization (WHO) in 1952 and used to the present day, is also the most cited public health definition in the global public health community.

According to "A Dictionary of Modern Preventive Medicine" published in 1998, edited by Shouyang Yu, public health is defined as: "*With society as the object, through administrative management, legal supervision, and promotional education, it coordinates social forces through macro-regulation to improve the sanitary condition of society and elevate the health level of the entire population. It is a social management function that reflects the close connection between medicine, socio-economic development, and social stability under modern social development conditions where people's health is increasingly becoming a societal issue.*"

According to "A Dictionary of Epidemiology (Sixth Edition)" edited by Miquel Porta, the definition of public health has four dimensions (Porta 2014). Public health is:

J. Liu, *Risk Management in Public Health*, Innovation in Risk Analysis,
https://doi.org/10.1007/978-981-97-6826-4_1

- *The health of a whole society. It can be measured and assessed through quantitative and qualitative indicators and analytic processes.*
- *The specific policies, services, programs and other essential efforts agreed (ideally, and often, democratically), organized, structured, financed, monitored, and evaluated by society to collectively protect, promote, and restore the people's health and its determinants.*
- *The institutions, public and private organizations—including private and public companies—, and other citizens organizations, that plan, develop, fund, and implement such efforts, and which are thus an integral part of local, national, regional, and global public health systems.*
- *The scientific disciplines and professions, knowledge, methods, art, and craft essential to positively influence health determinants, and thus prevent disease and disability, prolong life, and promote health through the organized and collective efforts of society.*

1.1.2 Characteristics of Public Health

1.1.2.1 Population-Based

Public health studies and understands health, disease, and health services from a population perspective, aiming to improve public health through group or societal measures.

1.1.2.2 Scientific Nature

The reliance on science makes public health distinct from general social activities, due to the application of knowledge from various disciplines to solve public health problems. Public health professionals regard epidemiology as their scientific core and collaborate across multiple disciplines, including preventive medicine, basic medicine, clinical medicine, and social sciences, to jointly tackle the various challenges.

1.1.2.3 Public Welfare Nature

Public health solely aims for the attainment of population health for the public. By strengthening the construction of public health systems, increasing the supply of public health products, and enhancing the quality of public health services, it thereby brings more health and welfare to the entire societal population.

1.1.2.4 Social Nature

Public health is inherently social, as public health issues can arise in any corner of society and, once they occur, they draw the attention of the entire community. Public health not only serves the public but also requires public participation.

1.2 Definition and Characteristics of Risk

Risk is omnipresent and ever-evolving, shifting alongside human development. The narrative of societal progression is intrinsically a history of contending with, countering, and managing risks. For millennia, humans did not ascribe a uniform nomenclature or understanding to the concept of risk. It was only within the past century or so that academia has provided a precise definition (Xu et al. 2016).

1.2.1 Concept of Risk

Drawing on social science research, the English word "risk" traces its etymology to the Italian word "risco," originally meaning "reef" or "rock," and subsequently evolved to convey the notion of danger. In the seventeenth century, this term entered the English linguistic framework through French and Italian influences.

1.2.1.1 Definition of Risk

The academic definition of risk originally stemmed from the insurance industry. In 1901, American scholar Allan H. Willett, in his doctoral thesis "*The Economic Theory of Risk and Insurance*", defined risk as "*the objective manifestation of the uncertainty of an event that is not desired to occur*" (Willett 1901). Subsequent to its initial conceptualization, the notion of risk has been sequentially researched and applied across various disciplines. Commencing in the 1930s, the food, pharmaceutical, and cosmetics industries began managing the permissible limits of toxic substances, reflecting an early application of risk in setting safety standards. The 1940s marked the advent of risk considerations in atomic energy and aerospace engineering safety management, wherein risk quantification was crucial for catastrophic event prevention. In the domain of economic crisis management, the 1970s further emphasized risk's pertinence in navigating fiscal turbulence. Additionally, disciplines such as psychology, sociology, and cultural studies started examining risk from social science vantage points, subsequently offering comprehensive recommendations.

In essence, the definition of risk across these fields essentially orbits around the "probability of incurring loss", albeit finely tuned to align with the specific application purposes and evaluative methodologies of each domain.

1.2.1.2 Changes in the Definition of Risk by the International Organization for Standardization (ISO)

In 1992, J. Frank Yates and Eric R. Stone proposed a three-factor model of risk structure, positing that risk comprises the potential for loss, the magnitude of the loss, and the uncertainty associated with the potential occurrence of loss. This triadic model captures the essence of risk and has become a foundational conceptual framework in modern risk theory.

In an effort to promote a uniform understanding of risk terminology across industries and organizations, the International Organization for Standardization (ISO) defined risk in its 2002 publication "Risk Management Vocabulary" as "*the combination of the probability of an event and its consequences*" (International Electrotechnical Commission 2002).

In 2009, ISO broadened the definition of risk to accommodate the needs of more industries and fields as "effect of uncertainty on objectives", which includes five aspects: (1) effects refer to deviation from the expected, which can be positive and/or negative; (2) there can be multiple objectives, applicable at different levels; (3) risk often has potential events and consequences or both features; (4) risk is often expressed as a combination of the consequences of an event (including changes in circumstances) and the associated likelihood of occurrence; (5) uncertainty is a state of limited or partial lack of information, understanding, or knowledge of an event, its consequences, or likelihood. Another important change was that the term "likelihood" was used to describe the probability of risk, replacing the previous "probability" used in the 2002 version, to avoid the narrow interpretation of risk probability as merely statistical probability. The 2022 version of "Risk Management Vocabulary" maintains the same basic definition of risk but includes more detailed descriptions in specific definitions (Golpayegani et al. 2022).

1.2.2 Characteristics of Risk (Xu et al. 2016)

1.2.2.1 Objectivity and Uncertainty

Whether and when risks occur, and the consequences thereof, are not subject to human will and possess objectivity. The occurrence of events, the subjects affected, the time and space, conditions of occurrence, and losses all have uncertainty. In conducting risk assessments, it is essential to recognize the existing uncertainties of the risks being assessed, to collect the latest and best evidence promptly, and to conduct dynamic assessments.

1.2.2.2 Relativity and Variability

The frequency and consequences of the same risk can vary for different participating entities, leading to varied impacts of the risk on different subjects. Even for the same entity, the impact can change over different periods. Risk is the uncertainty of damage that may be caused under specific natural and social environments. With changes in the environment and societal development, the types, nature, and extent of risk losses can change. The same disease or event can have different impacts in different regions and populations.

1.2.2.3 Harmfulness and Social Amplification

The occurrence of risk is always accompanied by corresponding losses, illustrating the harmfulness of risk. The social amplification of risk refers to the characteristic of risk being magnified in social continued propagation and communication due to interactive effects. Specifically, the flow of risk information in personal and group communication may generate secondary effects and further impact such as changes in knowledge and beliefs, the extent of economic impact, shifts in political demands and atmospheres, and the level of disturbance to social order, leading to changes in risk monitoring and management systems. These effects are further perceived and experienced by individuals and groups, thus propagating to a wider scope—including more distant regions or populations, causing more considerable impact. Therefore, in the process of risk assessment, in addition to considering the direct consequences of an event (such as health damage, economic property loss, emergency response costs, etc.), one must also seriously consider the potential indirect societal amplification effects.

1.2.2.4 The Measurability and Controllability of Risk

As human understanding and management levels continue to improve, it has been progressively recognized that the occurrence of risk follows certain patterns. This regularity offers a realistic possibility for humans to understand, assess, and manage risks. For instance, risks exhibit certain statistical regularities, making it possible to describe the frequency and magnitude of risk using tools such as probability theory and mathematical statistics, thereby quantifying risk through statistical law and trend analysis. Like other risks, a substantial number of public health risks can be mitigated through early risk identification, analysis, and the extensive use of health resources and control measures. For example, in large-scale events like the Olympic Games or during the management of natural disasters like earthquakes, risk identification, estimation, and the implementation of appropriate measures have effectively reduced risks.

1.3 Definition and Characteristics of Public Health Risk

To date, the global academic community has not converged on a universally accepted definition of risk applicable across various fields. With the acceleration of urbanization, increasing frequency of human mobility, frequent occurrences of natural disasters and epidemics, and the emergence of new pathogens, public health and population health are facing increasingly serious threats. Public health risks, especially on acute public health emergencies, have become a new challenge worldwide (Li et al. 2014).

1.3.1 Definition and Characteristics of Public Health Risk

The WHO defines acute public health risks in the "Rapid Risk Assessment of Acute Public Health Events" as "risks of acute (emergency) events causing negative impacts on public health". Public events are classified into infectious disease outbreaks, mass unexplained diseases, food safety and occupational hazards, events affecting public life safety, events affecting public health, and animal disease outbreaks. Based on the above definition, public health risk refers to the likelihood and consequences of events that may adversely affect public health. These events could be sudden, such as public health events, natural disasters, accident disasters, etc., or non-sudden, such as smoking, noise, indoor pollution, radiation, lifestyle behaviors, population mobility, etc. Besides the basic characteristics of risk, public health risks also involve multiple triggering factors, difficulty in initial recognition, complex mechanisms, and extensive impact.

The main public health risks the world currently faces include: health risks posed by natural disasters such as climate change; direct and indirect health risks resulting from environmental pollution; accelerated spread of infectious diseases due to increasingly frequent economic, social development, and population mobility; and the risk of cross-species transmission of infectious diseases caused by frequent and changing contact between humans and animals, and among animals themselves.

1.3.2 Definition and Characteristics of Risk in Public Health Emergencies

1.3.2.1 Definition of Risks in Public Health Emergencies

A public health emergency is defined as a sudden occurrence causing or likely to cause severe harm to the social public's physical and mental health. Public health emergencies can be classified into eight categories based on their causes: diseases caused by biological pathogens, mass poisoning caused by toxic and harmful factors, food poisoning events, natural disasters, occupational poisonings, accidents leading to death, unexplained mass illness or death, and terrorist events. Different countries may define and focus on public health emergencies differently, depending on the major health threats they face.

Risks in public health emergencies mainly denotes the probability and potential adverse outcomes arising from the previously detailed public health events, induced and derived from the aforementioned public health emergencies, that threaten the lives and health of the population and pollute and destroy the environment and resources, potentially causing direct, indirect health threats, and long-term impacts on humans.

1.3.2.2 Characteristics of Risks in Public Health Emergencies

In addition to the general characteristics of risk and public health risk, risks in public health emergencies also exhibit the following characteristics:

Diversity of Causes

Various natural disasters like earthquakes and floods can lead to risks in public health emergencies, such as environmental pollution, ecological destruction, traffic accident disasters, and other events that may endanger public health. Social safety incidents, such as biological terrorism, are also a significant cause of public health risks. Additionally, public health situations worsened by virulent infectious diseases, animal epidemics, pathogenic microbes, pharmaceutical hazards, food poisoning, occupational hazards, etc., can lead to an increased risk.

Variability in Distribution

The types of public health emergencies that occur can vary among different populations, regions, and time periods. Influenza, a highly contagious respiratory illness, has a marked seasonal pattern. In temperate regions, the peak of influenza activity usually occurs in winter and early spring. Health care workers are at higher risk of contracting diseases transmitted through blood and respiratory pathways than the general population. Urban populations, due to high density, limited living space, high mobility, and traffic congestion, are more prone to the spread of respiratory infections, while rural areas, with poorer sanitation and closer proximity to natural environments, are more susceptible to enteric infections, vector-borne diseases, and zoonotic diseases.

Severity of Impact on Public Psychology

Public health emergencies often have sudden, urgent, and rapid health impact characteristics. The public often lacks relevant emergency knowledge and psychological preparation. Pushed by media publicity and public opinion, the general public is more prone to panic, anxiety, unease, and tension.

Unpredictability of Harmful Consequences

The emergence of public health emergencies often has a gestation period, only evolving into an event under certain conditions. In the initial brewing stage, these are often not the focus of public attention.

1.4 Theories of Risk Assessment

Risk assessment, as a core component of risk management activities, is a crucial way for people to discover risks, understand risks, and subsequently take measures to eliminate and reduce risks, aiming to decrease the occurrence of risks and thereby avoid or mitigate the impact of risks on socioeconomic development (Xu et al. 2016; Zhu et al. 2017).

1.4.1 Concept and Significance of Risk Assessment

1.4.1.1 Historical Evolution of Risk Assessment

Risk assessment has been perfected alongside the constant improvement of risk management theory. Its prototype can be traced back to 916 BC, but it was not until the modern era that risk began to be studied as a discipline. In 1940, Dr. Lewis C. Robbins first proposed the concept of health risk assessment to guide effective disease prevention work. His pioneering health hazard chart was the world's earliest health risk assessment tool, giving medical examination results more disease predictive meanings. In the late 1960s, as life insurance actuarial methods were extensively applied to the quantitative estimation of individual patients' death risk probabilities, this greatly promoted the quantitative assessment of health risks, marking the discipline's transition into a phase of refinement and development. Since then, risk assessment has expanded from health risk assessment to the entire field of public health, receiving increasing attention. In 1983, the United States National Research Council (NRC) published a groundbreaking report named "Risk Assessment in the Federal Government: Managing the Process" in a government risk assessment report. It proposed a comprehensive management framework for assessing and managing health and environmental risks, the first structural systematic description of the health risk assessment and management process, which has been widely recognized globally.

Overall, health risk assessment relative to other fields' risk assessments commenced later, and theories and methods are lesser. Most of them use methods from other fields for health risk assessments, and work and research on public health risk assessment are still in the initial stages. Theories and methods for such assessments need further exploration and learning.

1.4.1.2 Concept of Risk Assessment

Risk assessment refers to the process of using scientific bases for decision-making needs to systematically use related information to identify the sources of risks with uncertainty and estimate those risks. It then compares the estimated risks against a given risk criterion to decide the severity of the risk. Risk assessment is a core part of risk management, including risk identification, risk analysis, and risk evaluation. Risk assessment activities are embedded in the risk management process, closely integrated, and mutually reinforcing with other risk management activities.

Risk assessment work attempts to answer the following basic questions: (1) What could happen and why (through risk identification)? What is the likelihood of it happening? What are the consequences? (2) Are there factors that can mitigate the consequences of the risk or lower the likelihood of risk occurrence? (3) Is the level of risk tolerable or acceptable? (4) Is further action and handling required?

1.4.1.3 Significance of Risk Assessment

The main functions of risk assessment include the following aspects: (1) To understand risks and their main causes, reveal weak links in the risk formation process, and clarify events needing priority treatment and their economically effective measures; (2) To help decision-makers accurately understand risks, assisting in selecting the best response strategies and measures; (3) To meet regulatory requirements; (4) To take targeted preventive measures.

Therefore, risk assessment is a prerequisite for avoiding and controlling risks, achieving risk control. Risk assessment can provide a quantitative basis for decision-makers to make decisions, and its assessment results can be used to determine the priority order of the measures to be taken.

1.4.2 Theories Related to Risk Assessment

1.4.2.1 Risk Theory

Risk theory reflects the basic content and characteristics of risk, providing a basic conceptual framework for risk management. Risk is generally considered to include three basic elements: adverse events, the probability of adverse events occurring, and the loss caused by adverse events. Here, the loss includes tangible objective losses (such as illness and casualties among personnel, economic loss, environmental impact, etc.) and intangible adverse losses (such as psychological impact on people, international impact and reputation, social impact, and political influence, etc.).

1.4.2.2 Data Inference Theory

Common foundational principles and theories include the Law of Large Numbers, principles of statistical inference, and the principle of inertia. The Law of Large Numbers refers to a series of theorems describing the stability of the average results of a large number of random phenomena, used in risk management to assess the probability of risk events occurring and the size of losses by utilizing the dialectical relationship between inevitability and randomness within the law of large numbers. With limited sample information, statistical inference principles are used to infer the overall situation and characteristics, and the principle of inertia is applied to analyze historical data to predict future risks and losses.

1.4.2.3 Risk Grading Theory

Risk grading theory involves using probability and mathematical statistical methods based on risk identification to perform quantitative analysis on the probability of a specific major infectious disease risk occurring and the severity of losses that may result from the epidemic. It estimates the probability of loss occurrence and the size of the loss; sorts risks according to vulnerability and risk tolerance ability, or calculates risk scores and ranks; and takes targeted management measures according to different risk grading scenarios.

1.4.2.4 Grey System Theory

Grey system theory is an analytic approach designed to investigate and resolve systems characterized by partially known and partially unknown information, referred to as grey systems. This theory offers a method for addressing system problems under conditions of scant information. Central to grey system theory is the concept of modeling based on limited information, where risk information is often incomplete or uncertain. For instance, in the initial stages of an emerging infectious disease outbreak, key information—such as the pathogen responsible, the incubation period, the transmissibility, the basic reproduction number, the rate of severe cases, and mortality rates—is typically scarce, representing a state of information deficiency. However, rapid decision-making is required for outbreak response, making grey system theory a valuable tool in the assessment and management of infectious disease risks.

The fundamental process of grey system theory involves the initial transformation of raw data using accumulation generation and reduction generation methods. Subsequently, a grey model, denoted as [GM(n,h)], is established based on the transformed data. The identified model undergoes precision tests such as residual testing, posterior difference test, or relevance test. When the accuracy meets the required standards, the [GM(n,h)] grey model can be employed for risk analysis.

With respect to risk assessment, grey assessment methods based on grey system theory are adapted to the specific goals and criteria of the evaluation. These may include grey relational pattern assessment, grey statistical evaluation, grey situation assessment, grey clustering evaluation, and multidimensional grey comprehensive evaluation, among others.

1.4.3 Methods of Risk Assessment

There are numerous widely utilized risk assessment methods globally. Generally, these are based on traditional statistical and analytical techniques, performing qualitative and quantitative analysis on relevant factors. Risk assessment methods quantify the likelihood and potential consequences of events in terms of a risk score to ascertain the level of risk, thereby offering decision-making recommendations for risk mitigation.

Various factors influence the choice of risk assessment techniques and methods. In practical application, considerations include: the complexity of the issue and the required analytical approach; the nature and extent of uncertainty in conducting the risk assessment; the level of resources needed, primarily regarding time, expertise, data demand, or costs; and whether the method can yield a quantitative result. In complex situations, it may be necessary to employ multiple assessment techniques and methods concurrently.

1.5 Approaches of Public Health Risk Management

Risk management is a systematic, professional, scientific, and comprehensive task. It is an essential foundation for implementing the principle of "prevention first, proactive measures" in public health risk prevention and control. It is also a scientifically-based management tool that enhances the predictability, specificity, and scientific rigor of public health risk prevention and control efforts.

1.5.1 Definition and Process of Public Health Risk Management

Public health risk management is the decision-making process used by social organizations or individuals to reduce the negative outcomes of sudden public health risks. This process includes risk identification, risk assessment, and risk evaluation. Based on these, various risk management techniques are selected and optimized to effectively control risks and appropriately handle the consequences of losses caused by risks, achieving maximum safety assurance at the minimum cost. The ultimate aim of risk management is to implement activities following risk assessment and integrate them with risk management efforts to ensure preparedness and efficient response.

According to the lifecycle of risk, risk management can be divided into several basic segments: planning and preparation, risk identification, risk estimation, risk evaluation, and risk disposal. These segments are cyclically repeated, thus forming a complete, continuous, and dynamic risk management process (Fig. 1.1) (Zhu et al. 2017).

a. Planning and Preparation

The first step of risk management is planning and preparation. This involves understanding the internal and external environment of the organization, establishing risk assessment standards, and ensuring risk management support.

b. Risk Identification

Risk identification is the process by which epidemiologists and managers judge and categorize both existing and potential risks, and assess the nature of these risks.

c. Risks Estimation

Risk estimation is based on risk identification and involves analyzing a large amount of detailed loss data collected. Using probability theory and mathematical statistics, the probability and extent of risk occurrence are estimated and predicted. Risk estimation primarily includes the frequency and severity of losses.

d. Risk Management Methods

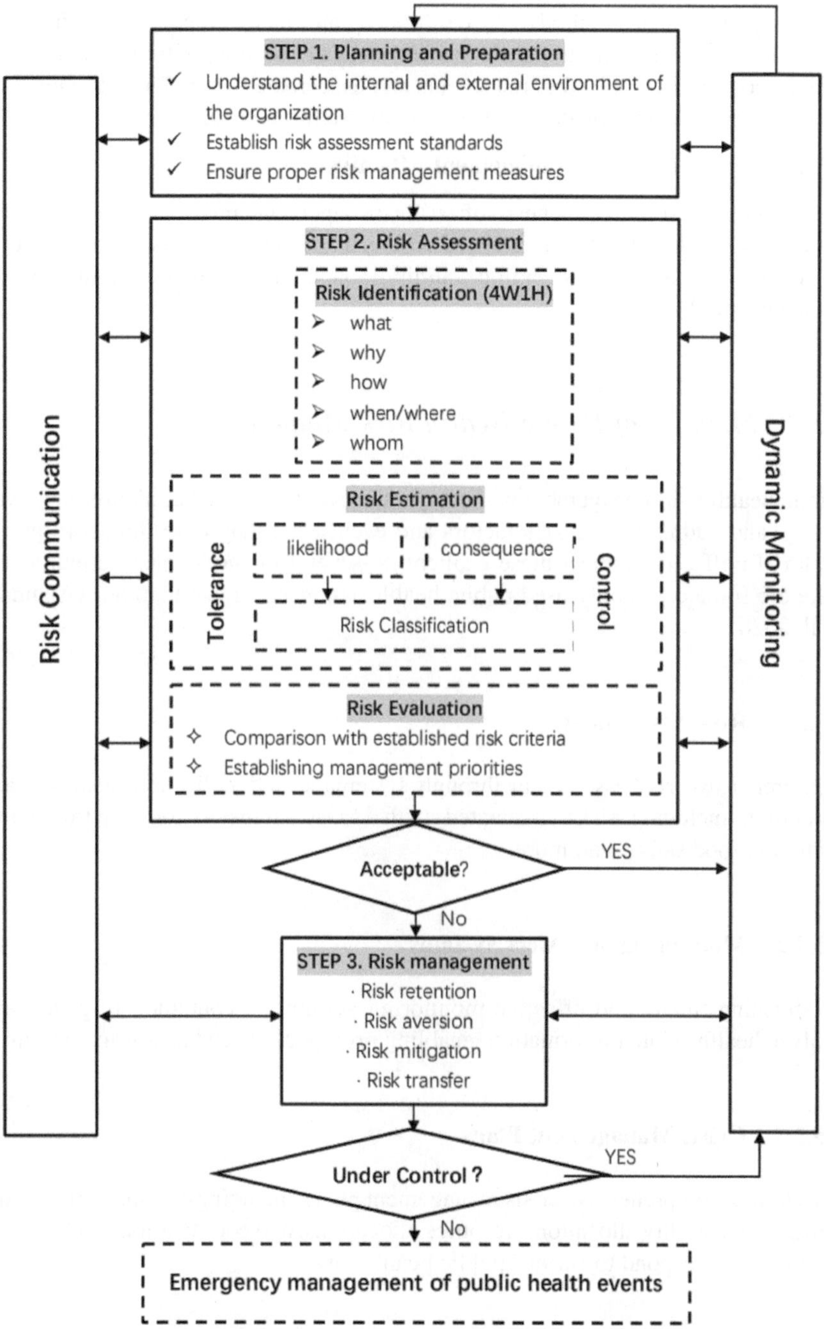

Fig. 1.1 Basic process of public health risk management

Risk management methods can be divided into control methods and financial methods. The former aims to reduce the frequency and severity of losses by changing various conditions that lead to risk events and exacerbate losses. The latter involves financial arrangements made in advance to absorb the costs of risks.

e. Evaluation of Risk Management Effectiveness

Evaluating the effectiveness of risk management involves analyzing and comparing the results of implemented risk management methods to the expected objectives, assessing the scientific validity, adaptability, and profitability of the management plan.

1.5.2 Methods of Public Health Risk Management

Public health risk management is a comprehensive task, aimed at identifying, evaluating, and addressing various factors and events that may pose threats to public health. To effectively meet these challenges, several methods must be employed. Here are some commonly used public health risk management methods (Alauddin et al. 2020):

1.5.2.1 Risk Assessment

Comprehensive risk assessment through systematic data collection, analysis, and modeling, including risks associated with disease transmission, environmental pollution, food safety, and more.

1.5.2.2 Monitoring and Alert Systems

Establishing timely and effective monitoring systems to continuously gather and analyze health-related information, enabling prompt alerts and necessary actions.

1.5.2.3 Crisis Management Plans

Developing comprehensive crisis management plans, including organizational structures, responsibility allocations, resource allocations, and coordination mechanisms, to effectively respond to various public health crises.

1.5.2.4 Risk Communication

Creating open and transparent risk communication mechanisms to convey risk information to the public, governmental agencies, and other stakeholders, enhancing public awareness, understanding, and promoting collaborative actions.

1.5.2.5 Intervention Measures

Formulating and implementing appropriate intervention measures based on risk assessment results, such as vaccination, health education, and environmental improvements, to reduce or eliminate public health risks.

1.5.2.6 Ongoing Oversight and Evaluation

Regularly supervising and evaluating public health risk management measures, adjusting and improving strategies and actions timely to ensure their effectiveness and timeliness.

1.5.2.7 Cross-Sectoral Collaboration

Strengthening cooperation and coordination between government departments, academic institutions, healthcare facilities, community organizations, and international organizations to collectively address public health risks, achieving resource and information sharing.

References

Alauddin M, Khan MAI, Khan F et al (2020) How can process safety and a risk management approach guide pandemic risk management? J Loss Prev Process Ind 68:104310

Golpayegani D, Pandit HJ, Lewis D (2022) Airo: an ontology for representing ai risks based on the proposed eu ai act and iso risk management standards[M]//Towards a Knowledge-Aware AI. IOS Press, pp 51–65.

International Electrotechnical Commission (2002) Risk management-vocabulary-guidelines for use in standards. International Organization for Standardization (ISO)

Li B, Wu QH, Kang Z et al (2014) Theory and technical guide of public health risk assessment for emergency events. People's Medical Publishing House, Beijing

Porta M (2014) A dictionary of epidemiology. Oxford University Press

Willett AH (1901) The economic theory of risk and insurance. Columbia University Press

Xu SQ, Wang Y, Wang W et al (2016) Theory and practice of public health risk assessment for emergency events. People's Medical Publishing House, Beijing

Zhu FC, Shen XB, Jin H et al (2017) Theory and practice of public health emergency response. Southeast University Press, Nanjing

Chapter 2
Theory and Approaches of Public Health Risk Assessment for Emerging Infectious Diseases

2.1 Outbreaks and Threats of Emerging Infectious Diseases

2.1.1 Background

Before the twentieth century, infectious diseases were the most important diseases endangering human health and affecting social stability, and every time they appeared in history, they brought great disasters to mankind. After entering the 21th century, with the development of social economy, the progress of medical technology, and the promotion of public health measures, the incidence and mortality of infectious diseases in most countries around the world have decreased significantly. Although infectious diseases are no longer the leading cause of death, due to the increasingly close human interaction, a series of chain reactions caused by climate change, the destruction of human ecological environment and changes in behavior patterns, various emerging infectious diseases continue to appear, posing a great threat to human health and posing new challenges to global public health.

Emerging infectious diseases indicate infectious disease that is newly emerging in a population, or that is rapidly increasing in incidence or rapidly expanding in endemic areas. Through the analysis of about 335 new infectious disease events that appeared in the world from 1940 to 2004, researchers have found that most of the emerging infectious diseases are zoonotic diseases, and the vast majority of these zoonotic diseases (71.8%) are caused by wildlife pathogens, such as Ebola, severe acute respiratory syndrome (SARS), avian influenza, etc. (Jones et al. 2008). Michael et al. amassed a dataset from the literature that contains 2938 observations of infectious disease responses to global change drivers across 1497 host–parasite combinations, including plant, animal and human hosts (Mahon et al. 2024). They found that biodiversity loss, chemical pollution, climate change and introduced species are associated with increases in disease-related end points or harm, indicating that reducing greenhouse gas emissions, managing ecosystem health, and preventing biological invasions and biodiversity loss could help to reduce the burden of plant,

J. Liu, *Risk Management in Public Health*, Innovation in Risk Analysis,
https://doi.org/10.1007/978-981-97-6826-4_2

animal and human diseases, especially when coupled with improvements to social and economic determinants of health (Mahon et al. 2024). Less than half way into the twenty-first century, human beings have already experienced several epidemics of emerging infectious diseases. Their wide spread, large number of infected people and rapid spread have become a public health problem of global concern.

2.1.2 *Types of Emerging Infectious Diseases*

To be specific, the Emerging infectious diseases in general can be divided into the following five classes according to the pathogen found situation (Lu and Liang 2018):

A. Infectious diseases caused by newly emerging pathogens, such as severe acute respiratory syndrome (SARS), Middle East respiratory syndrome (MERS), coronavirus disease 2019 (COVID-19).
B. Infectious diseases newly diagnosed with known pathogens, such as human immune deficiency virus infection or acquired immune deficiency syndrome (HIV/AIDS), cervical cancer.
C. Recurrence of infectious diseases, i.e. infectious diseases that have been controlled and have important public health impact have epidemics or outbreaks again (such as syphilis, gonorrhea);
D. Infectious diseases caused by emergence of new drug-resistant pathogens, such as the drug-resistant tuberculosis.
E. Infectious diseases input from outside. Specifically, it means that a type of infectious diseases that a country or region has not been found or has eliminated break out due to the pathogens imported from abroad (such as wild virus polio).

2.1.3 *Global Disease Burden of Emerging Infectious Diseases*

Driven by the WHO's objective of eliminating some infectious diseases such as tuberculosis, viral hepatitis and AIDS, the world has made some progress in its efforts to address various infectious diseases. However, on the whole, the disease burden of infectious diseases faced globally is still relatively serious. The challenges of responding to, preventing and controlling infectious diseases remain enormous.

2.1.3.1 Tuberculosis and Drug-Resistant Tuberculosis

Tuberculosis (TB) is a preventable and usually curable disease. Human have been fighting with them for thousands of years. Yet in 2022, TB was the world's second leading cause of death from a single infectious agent, after COVID-19, and caused almost twice as many deaths as HIV/AIDS. In view of the emergence of drug-resistant strains, tuberculosis remains a major global public health problem.

The reported global number of people newly diagnosed with TB was 7.5 million in 2022 (World Health Organization 2023). This is the highest number since WHO began global TB monitoring in 1995, above the pre-COVID baseline (and previous historical peak) of 7.1 million in 2019, and up from 5.8 million in 2020 and 6.4 million in 2021. The number in 2022 probably includes a sizeable backlog of people who developed TB in previous years, but whose diagnosis and treatment was delayed by COVID-related disruptions that affected access to and provision of health services. Globally, the estimated TB incidence rate (new cases per 100 000 population per year) was 133 (95% uncertain interval [UI]: 124–143) in 2022. The net reduction from 2015 to 2022 was 8.7%, far from the WHO End TB Strategy milestone of a 50%. Globally in 2022, TB caused an estimated 1.30 million deaths (95% UI: 1.18–1.43 million). This was down from best estimates of 1.4 million in both 2020 and 2021 and almost back to the level of 2019.

Drug-resistant TB continues to be a public health threat. Resistance to rifampicin–the most effective firstline drug—is of greatest concern. TB that is resistant to rifampicin and isoniazid is defined as multidrug-resistant TB (MDR-TB). Both MDR-TB and rifampicin-resistant TB (RR-TB) require treatment with second-line drugs. Globally, an estimated 410 000 people (95% UI: 370 000–450 000) developed multidrug-resistant or rifampicin-resistant TB (MDR/RR-TB) in 2022. The highest proportions (>50% of previously treated cases with MDR/RR-TB) are found in the Russian Federation and in several countries in Eastern Europe and Central Asia. Noticeably, only 825 000 of people with MDR/RR-TB have been treated between 2018 and 2022, achieving 55% targets set at the 2018 United Nations (UN) high-level meeting on TB. Additionally, about 50% of TB patients and their households face total costs (direct medical expenditures, non-medical expenditures and indirect costs such as income losses) that are catastrophic (>20% of annual household income), far from the WHO End TB Strategy target of zero. This shows that there are major economic and financial barriers to accessing and completing TB treatment, which need to be addressed through faster progress towards universal health coverage (UHC) and better levels of social protection.

2.1.3.2 Viral Hepatitis

Improved data from 187 countries shows that viral hepatitis is a major public health challenge of this decade. The estimated number of people newly infected by viral hepatitis declined from 2.5 million in 2019 to 2.2 million in 2022 (World Health Organization 2024). Of these, 1.2 million are hepatitis B infections and nearly 1.0 million are hepatitis C infections.

Viral hepatitis is one of the communicable diseases for which mortality is increasing. An estimated 1.3 million people died from viral hepatitis in 2022. Of the 1.3 million deaths, hepatitis B caused 1.1 million deaths and hepatitis C 244

000 deaths. Viral hepatitis and tuberculosis were the second leading causes of death among communicable diseases in 2022, after COVID-19.

Ten countries account for nearly two thirds of the global burden of viral hepatitis B and C: China, India, Indonesia, Nigeria, Pakistan, Ethiopia, Bangladesh, Viet Nam, Philippines and the Russian Federation. There is regional variation in the viral hepatitis burden and response. The WHO African Region accounts for 63% of new hepatitis B infections, but only 18% of newborns in the Region receive the hepatitis B birth-dose vaccination. The Western Pacific Region accounts for 47% of hepatitis B deaths, and treatment coverage remains low.

High-impact interventions are available, such as an effective cure for hepatitis C and vaccines for hepatitis B, but access to these interventions must be urgently expanded to save lives and prevent a future generation of new infections, cancers and deaths.

2.1.3.3 Aids

AIDS remains a major global public health issue, with sustained transmission in all countries around the world and some countries reporting increasing trends in new infections when previously on the decline. In 2022, 630 000 (480 000–880 000) people died from HIV-related causes and 1.3 million (1.0–1.7 million) people acquired HIV (World Health Organization n.d.). There were an estimated 39.0 million (33.1–45.7 million) people living with HIV at the end of 2022, two thirds of whom (25.6 million) are in the WHO African Region. HIV has claimed 40.4 million (32.9–51.3 million) lives so far with ongoing transmission in all countries globally.

2.2 Emerging Infectious Diseases Related Risk Assessment Theories

Infectious disease emergency is one of the most common public health emergencies, and it is one of the most concerned emergencies of the society. In recent years, the sudden, frequent, and high incidence of emerging infectious diseases not only seriously affect social stability and economic development, but also pose a great threat to human health. Timely and effective risk assessment of emerging infectious diseases will help to prevent and control the epidemic, minimize the public health harms caused by the epidemic of emerging infectious diseases, maintain social stability, and ensure public health.

2.2.1 Characteristics of Emerging Infectious Disease Emergencies

In addition to the general characteristics of emergencies, emerging infectious diseases also have the following specific characteristics because of their epidemic characteristics (Xu and Wang 2017):

2.2.1.1 Seasonality and Regionality

Because the reproduction of pathogens or the activity and quantity fluctuation of host and vector insects are significantly affected by climatic conditions such as temperature and humidity, the occurrence of emerging infectious disease emergencies has obvious seasonality. For example, insect-borne infectious diseases have strict seasonal characteristics, mainly in summer and autumn seasons. The strains and vectors of emerging infectious diseases in different regions are not the same, even if the same disease has different characteristics in different regions, which leads to the regional characteristics of some emerging infectious diseases. For instance, dengue fever is mostly distributed in tropical areas, and Ebola hemorrhagic fever is mainly concentrated in Africa. It should be noted that the seasonal and regional nature of emerging infectious disease emergencies will also be affected by human production activities, customs, and changes in population susceptibility.

2.2.1.2 Periodicity

The prevalence of some emerging infectious diseases often shows regular changes after a specific time interval. When the emerging infectious diseases are in the high incidence period, the corresponding infectious disease emergencies will increase significantly. The periodic changes of emerging infectious diseases are more common in respiratory infectious diseases, which is caused by changes in population susceptibility and pathogen variation. If the effective immunity of the human body after influenza infection is not long, after 2–3 years the same type of influenza may re-circulate. Influenza viruses mutate frequently, and a larger influenza pandemic may emerge after 10–15 years.

2.2.1.3 Complexity

Due to the different pathogenic characteristics and invasion routes of different pathogens, the incidence of infection and emergencies are also significantly different under the influence of host, environment, and other drivers. At the same time, the clinical manifestations of different infectious diseases are diversified and complicated, such as the symptoms of a certain infectious disease may contain fever, rash, digestive system and other manifestations at the same time, or different infectious diseases may show similar symptoms. In addition, the course of the same type of infectious disease can also be manifested as acute, subacute, chronic and other characteristics. Some infectious diseases have mature measures of diagnosis, treatment, and prevention, while others have no specific diagnostic methods, therapeutic drugs, and available vaccines. These factors make the occurrence and development of emerging infectious disease emergencies more complicated than other types of emergencies.

2.2.1.4 Easy to Spread

The main difference between infectious diseases and other diseases is their infectivity. For emerging infectious diseases, people are generally susceptible to them, and once the diseases occur, they can spread rapidly and continuously. If effective control measures are not taken in time, it is very easy to cause cluster outbreaks and even epidemics, or even large-scale epidemics.

2.2.1.5 Suddenness

The "suddenness" of emerging infectious disease emergencies is more reflected in acute infectious diseases, such as the severe acute respiratory syndrome coronavirus 2 has high infectivity and short incubation period, and once it occurs in a collective environment, it can quickly cause hundreds of people to fall ill. It should be noted that some chronic infectious diseases, such as tuberculosis, are prone to occur in collective units such as boarding schools and detention centers where the accommodation environment is poor, because of its long incubation period and the initial symptoms are not obvious, so the development of the event is slower and difficult to be found in time. And once it is found, the epidemic of tuberculosis is often clustered, so it cannot deny its "sudden" characteristics.

2.2.1.6 Severity

The severity of the harm of emerging infectious disease emergencies, on the one hand, is reflected in the harm to public health and life, on the other hand, is reflected in the impact on social stability and economic development. The former is a direct hazard, and the latter is an indirect hazard, which should both be considered in the risk assessment of emerging infectious diseases. For example, in 2013, human infection with H7N9 bird flu was reported to have a case fatality rate of more than 30% and resulted in hundreds of billions of yuan in economic losses for the poultry industry.

2.2.1.7 Public Properties

The impact of emerging infectious disease emergencies is widespread. Most of the objects threatened by the outbreak and epidemic of emerging infectious diseases are specific groups of people in a specific time and environment, but sometimes due to inadequate control measures, the spread of infectious diseases will spread to other non-specific social groups, causing widespread impact. For example, COVID-19 in 2020 has swept the world, affecting tens of thousands of people.

2.2.1.8 Difficulty in Prediction

The occurrence of emerging infectious diseases is contingent, and it is difficult for us to accurately predict when, where and in what form infectious diseases will occur. For most emergencies, the casualties and social and economic losses can be assessed within a short time after the occurrence of the incident. However, emerging infectious diseases are characterized by rapid transmission and diffusion, and increasingly close interpersonal communication brings more opportunities for the spread of infectious diseases. Therefore, it is difficult to accurately predict the occurrence and development of infectious disease events regardless of specific prevention and control measures, and the prevention and control of such events are also full of uncertainties.

2.2.2 Characteristics of Risk Assessment for Emerging Infectious Diseases

In view of the characteristics of emerging infectious diseases, such as easy spread, great damage to health, complexity, and difficulty to predict, the public health risk assessment of emerging infectious diseases should fully consider the disease manifestations and harm characteristics, and carry out targeted analysis and evaluation. Therefore, the public health risk assessment of emerging infectious diseases has the following characteristics (Xu and Wang 2017):

2.2.2.1 Complexity of Consideration

The new process of the spread of infectious diseases including the source of infection, route of transmission and susceptible population, so the risk assessment of emerging infectious diseases shall consider the discovery of the source of infection control and feasibility, degree of difficulty of transmission to realize and control effect and susceptible people exposed opportunity and protective measures. From the perspective of one health, the epidemic process of infectious diseases includes pathogen, host, and environment, so the risk assessment must consider the invasion, infectivity and variation of the pathogen, the resistance of the host to the pathogen, and the adaptability of the pathogen and the host to the environment. In addition, because the characteristics of different types of emerging infectious diseases are not the same, the factors to be considered and the analysis points of different types of emerging infectious diseases cannot be generalized, especially parasitic, insect-borne, and natural infectious diseases, and the role of intermediate hosts and vectors in the transmission process should also be considered.

2.2.2.2 Staged Assessment Activities

In view of the diffusivity, harmfulness of emerging infectious diseases, the public health risk should be assessed sooner rather than later. At the same time, because of the different hazard characteristics of the different stages of the development of emerging infectious diseases, it is necessary to repeatedly assess the development process. According to the characteristics of different time risk assessment, the risk assessment of emerging infectious diseases can be divided into initial rapid assessment, phased assessment and terminal assessment.

2.2.2.3 Diversification of Evaluation Purposes

Before the occurrence of an emerging infectious disease event, daily risk assessment can be carried out based on daily surveillance data to detect the signs of an emerging infectious disease outbreak/epidemic in time. In the early stage of the development, it is necessary to timely analyze the various links and epidemic factors of the infectious disease transmission, study and judge the possibility of the spread of the infectious disease and the expansion of the harm, find the key points of risk control measures, and control the further spread. In the later stage of the development and after the event, it is necessary to evaluate the chronic effect and long-term harm of the infectious disease event, and propose normal long-term risk control measures. At the same time, it is necessary to draw lessons from the past, propose long-term measures to prevent similar events, and evaluate its implementation feasibility and prevention effect.

2.2.2.4 Internationalization of Evaluation Objects

In recent years, there have been frequent outbreaks of emerging infectious diseases, which often develop into global pandemics, causing great impact in the international community. Modern society has convenient transportation, close people-to-people contacts and frequent international exchanges, which greatly increase the chance of transnational transmission of infectious diseases. Therefore, the target of risk assessment of emerging infectious diseases is not limited to the common infectious diseases in the region or the country, but should also focus on the world.

2.2.3 *Theories Related to Risk Assessment of Emerging Infectious Diseases*

2.2.3.1 Three-Step Two-Factor Theory

Three-Step Two-Factor theory indicates the popular process of infectious disease and its influencing factors, including the source of infection, route of transmission and susceptible population three basic steps as well as the natural factors and social factors. Infectious source refers to the body of the pathogen growth, reproduction, and excretion of the pathogen people and animals, including patients with infectious diseases, pathogen carriers and infected animals. The period from the host infection to the appearance of clinical symptoms or signs is called the incubation period, and some pathogen carriers can excrete the pathogen at the end of the incubation period and are infectious. Transmission route refers to the whole process of the pathogen in the external environment after it is discharged from the infectious source and before it invades a new susceptible host. According to different media, transmission routes can be divided into air transmission, water transmission, food transmission, contact transmission, arthropod transmission, vertical transmission, etc. Susceptible population refers to the population that is sensitive to the invasion and spread of pathogens, and the degree of susceptibility depends on the proportion of susceptible people in the population. Natural factors and social factors are the key conditions affecting the spread of pathogens. Based on the theory of "Three-Step Two-Factor", risk assessment can be carried out according to the epidemic process of infectious diseases and its influencing factors, the possibility and intensity of pathogen transmission in the population can be analyzed, and feasible measures can be put forward to control each step and factor.

2.2.3.2 Triangle Model Theory (Liu et al. 2023)

During the responding to the COVID-19 pandemic, researchers have observed that the traditional "Three-Step Two-Factor" theory is not sufficient to meet the contemporary societal needs for newly emerging infectious disease prevention and control, and the "triangle model" theory (Fig. 2.1) came into being. The three elements of infectious disease transmission principle (infectivity, pathogenicity, virulence, source of infection, transmission route, susceptible population, etc.), health system's prevention and treatment capabilities (surveillance and early warning, screening, diagnosis, public health intervention, clinical treatment, etc.) and the public health and social measures (protection of key populations, management of key places, community governance, etc.) constitute a triangle. From a macro perspective, the "triangle model" theory not only considers the transmission law of infectious diseases themselves, but also evaluates the prevention and control capacity of the health system and public health and social measures, and comprehensively evaluates the epidemic risk of emerging infectious diseases. Since the epidemic of diseases, the prevention and

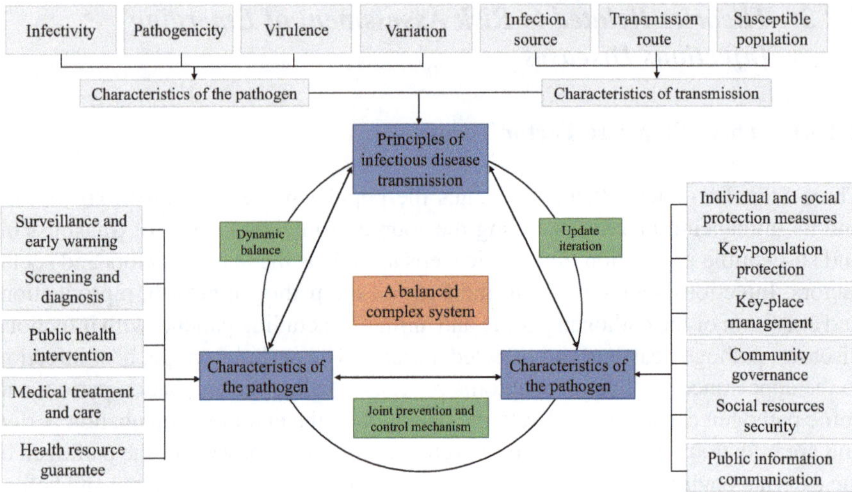

Fig. 2.1 The theory of "triangle model" for prevention and control of newly emerging infectious diseases

control capacity of the health system, and public health and social measures are all in dynamic development, the triangular model theory can be used to conduct real-time dynamic risk assessment of the epidemic of emerging infectious diseases, identify the weak links, make timely adjustments, and finally achieve triangular stability.

2.2.3.3 Health System Resilience Theory (Haldane et al. 2021)

The health system resilience theory (Fig. 2.2) is a theoretical framework for evaluating the resilience of health system formed by Victoria Haldane et al. based on the WHO health system framework adding public health functions and other contents. It mainly includes elements such as community engagement, health service delivery, public health function, medical products and technologies, health workforce, government and finance, cross-sectoral cooperation, and health equity and outcomes. Among them, community engagement is the core element, including health service delivery, public health functions, medical products and technologies, health workforce, government and funding, and other health sector related elements. The elements of intersectoral collaboration are those in which health and non-health sectors work together to address the social determinants of health. Underpinning these elements are health equity and health outcomes, where resilient health systems aim to produce positive physical and mental health outcomes for the entire population. Health resilience theory focuses on the comprehensive evaluation of health systems to assess their ability to respond to emerging infectious diseases, and thus indirectly analyze the risk of disease transmission and epidemic.

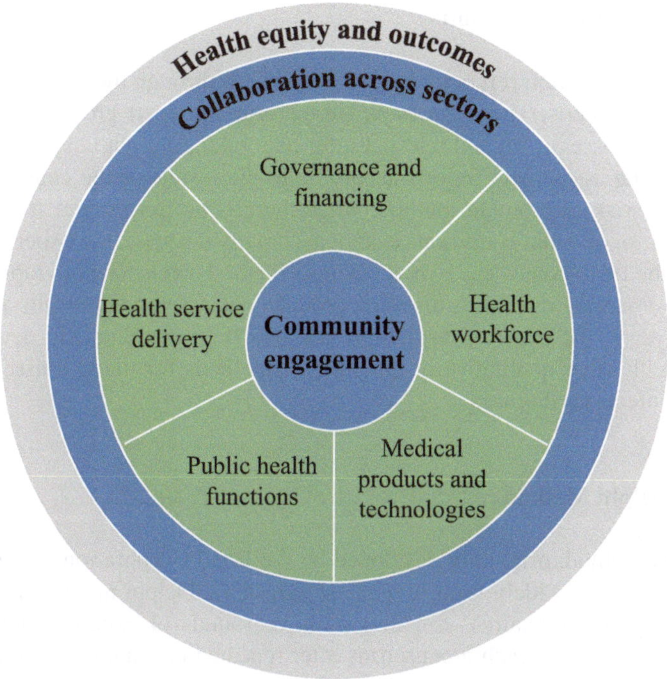

Fig. 2.2 Health systems resilience framework

2.2.4 Methods for Risk Assessment of Emerging Infectious Diseases

There are many kinds of risk assessment methods for emerging infectious diseases, and the specific method to carry out risk assessment needs to be comprehensively considered in combination with the background of risk management process and available risk assessment techniques. For different types of emerging infectious diseases, the pathogen characteristics are different, the mode of transmission is different, and the risk is very different, so the risk assessment usually involves the comprehensive application of multidisciplinary methods.

In the first chapter, we briefly summarize the commonly used method of public health risk assessment. In this chapter, we focus on common methods of risk assessment for emerging infectious diseases (Xu and Wang 2017; Wu et al. 2014; Liu 2023).

2.2.4.1 Expert Consultation

The expert consultation refers to the risk assessment through the form of collective discussion of experts. The main steps are to form an expert group, introduce the content of risk assessment and relevant information, discuss with experts, and write and submit the assessment reports according to the results of the consultation. As a qualitative risk assessment method, when there is no assessment framework or tool to refer to, or when conditions cannot accurately evaluate, the expert method is generally the first choice. The expert business method can be used to rapidly assess the risk of emerging infectious diseases, produce risk assessment results and report. In recent years, the expert consultation has also been continuously developed to combine with other qualitative or quantitative methods for the risk assessment of emerging infectious diseases.

2.2.4.2 Delphi Method

The Delphi method, originally developed by the Rand Corporation for technology forecasting, is now widely used in medical industries. Delphi method uses a series of structured questionnaires, conducts multiple rounds of expert evaluation, and finally makes experts reach a consensus after repeated consultation, induction and modification. Delphi method is often used in the construction of risk assessment index system, and has been applied to the establishment of risk assessment index system of respiratory diseases at frontier ports, infectious diseases after natural disasters, AIDS, infectious diseases on international cruise ships, etc. The Delphi method can also be used to estimate the risk of emerging infectious diseases. In recent years, Delphi method is often combined with other qualitative or quantitative methods such as risk matrix method to make the risk assessment index system of emerging infectious diseases more scientific.

2.2.4.3 Analytic Hierarchy Process

Analytic Hierarchy Process (AHP) is a kind of multi-criteria decision-making method which combines qualitative analysis and quantitative analysis, and is widely used. It divides complex problems into multiple levels, compares the importance of different elements in each level in pairs, establishes a judgment matrix, and obtains the weight of elements in each layer by calculating the eigen roots and vectors of the matrix, to make decisions according to the weight. The main steps of AHP are: establishing hierarchical structure model, comparing each layer element in pairs, constructing judgment matrix, judgment weight and consistency test. AHP helps to quantify the relative importance of indicators in effect evaluation, make the established effect evaluation index system more objective and credible, increase the gap between the weights of different indicators, and reduce the computational complexity caused by too many variables. AHP is often combined with Delphi method to construct an evaluation index system for the risk or prevention and control effect of emerging infectious diseases. The indexes to be evaluated are selected by Delphi method, and the weights of each index are quantitatively calculated by AHP method. In recent years, there are also studies that combine AHP with expert consultation and risk matrix method to assess the risk and prevention and control effect of emerging infectious diseases.

2.2.4.4 Risk Matrix Method

Risk matrix refers to a risk management tool method that draws risks in matrix according to the possibility of risk occurrence and the severity of the consequences of risk occurrence, and shows the risk and its importance level. The collected data and evaluation results can be applied in the entire risk management process. Risk matrix method refers to the quantitative scoring of the occurrence possibility and consequence severity of risk factors determined by experienced experts, and the scoring results are included in the two-dimensional matrix table for calculation, and finally the risk level is obtained. The WHO's Rapid Risk Assessment for Public Health Emergencies presents a risk hierarchy matrix, with green, yellow, orange, and red indicating low, medium, high, and very high risks. The risk matrix must have the ability to identify the risk factors in the whole event, that is, in the process of building the whole model, it should be constructed according to the possibility of actual occurrence of risks (referred to as occurrence probability, set as L) and the severity of consequences caused by the occurrence of risks (referred to as impact degree, set as S). The risk value $R = L \times S$. At the same time, the corresponding quantification is processed and analyzed. The larger the R-value, the greater the risk in this link, and effective measures must be taken.

Risk matrix method is a common risk classification method, which has been applied to the risk assessment of imported infectious diseases, respiratory infectious diseases, post-flood infectious diseases, insect-borne infectious diseases, etc. Risk matrix method is often combined with Delphi method and expert consultation to assess the risk of emerging infectious diseases. In 2019, the European Centre for Disease Prevention and Control (ECDC) has published the Operational Tool on Rapid Assessment Methodology, which uses a risk matrix approach. Rapid risk assessment is carried out through five main steps: defining risk problems, collecting and testing risk information, systematically collecting and extracting literature information, evaluating evidence, and assessing risks, which not only provides reference for experts engaged in rapid risk assessment of infectious diseases at the national or regional level, but also provides reference for experts engaged in rapid risk assessment of infectious diseases.

2.2.4.5 Mathematical or Probabilistic Models

To study the spread speed, spatial range and transmission mechanism of infectious diseases and guide the effective prevention and control of infectious diseases, researchers have established several mathematical models. In according to the types of infectious diseases, common models can be divided into susceptible infected (SI) model, susceptible infected recovered (SIR) model, susceptible infected recovered susceptible (SIRS) model, susceptible exposed infected recovered (SEIR) model, etc. These models have also been applied to the risk prediction of infectious diseases such as Ebola and COVID-19.

In the prediction and risk assessment of infectious diseases, Markov chain, Monte Carlo simulation, Bayesian statistics and Bayesian networks, Markov chain Monte Carlo method are several commonly used evaluation methods based on probabilistic statistical models. At present, many studies have applied them to the prediction and quantitative risk assessment of infectious diseases, among which Monte Carlo simulation and Markov chain Monte Carlo method can also be used to estimate parameters in complex prediction models. In recent years, some studies have established dynamic infectious disease models for more timely monitoring and early warning of infectious diseases.

2.2.4.6 Scenario Analysis

Scenario analysis refers to the method of analyzing the various scenarios that may occur in the future and the possible impacts of various scenarios by means of hypothesis, simulation and prediction. Scenario analysis assumes that the future development is diversified. Through scenario analysis, we can have a more intuitive understanding of the uncertainty of the future, and urge decision-makers to consider which scenarios may occur (such as the best scenario, the worst scenario, and the expected scenario), which helps decision-makers to fully prepare for the possible scenarios in advance. The basic process includes:

A. Clarify the goal and determine the focus of decision-making. The focus problem should have two characteristics: importance and uncertainty.
B. Identify key risk factors and their uncertainties. List, analyze and compare all risk factors, identify and record risk sources, risk events and risk symptoms, and rank these risk factors according to the degree of impact and uncertainty of risks.
C. Establish a scenario framework, based on the occurrence, development and evolution of major infectious disease outbreaks, and build and develop a series of scenarios by "pushing forward" based on the main framework of scenario content.
D. Simulation scenario. Select and determine several scenarios, analyze the key factors of each scenario, fully consider all possible details in the scenario, and form a series of comprehensive, detailed and reasonable "stories". The "story" is thoroughly analyzed and the influence brought by the "story" is analyzed.

E. Development of "scenario-response" decision scheme. Based on different scenarios, a reasonable "scenario-response" decision scheme should be developed, and the focus problem or coping strategy of each scenario is evaluated to select the optimal strategy. The key points of the scenario-response strategy analysis include changes in external circumstances, the possible different consequences of the decisions to be made, and the needs and possible changes of stakeholders. When the situation is changing, some early monitoring indicators can be identified to reflect the change, so that timely response can be made.
F. To put forward policy recommendations and action plans. In recent years, some scholars and professionals have realized scenario analysis and simulation through sand table exercises, such as the scenario analysis of influenza pandemic and unknown infectious disease pandemic X.

2.2.4.7 Comprehensive Risk Assessment

Comprehensive risk assessment refers to the assessment of risk using a combination of multiple methods, multiple resources and multiple monitoring measures. Because any approach has certain limitations, a combination of different approaches can help capture different aspects of a risk problem. Especially in the early stage of the epidemic of major emerging infectious diseases with very limited information, it is a better choice to integrate multiple risk assessment techniques to conduct comprehensive risk assessment from multidisciplinary perspectives such as epidemiology, clinical medicine, management, sociology, economics and communication to better carry out risk assessment work. In the practical application process of comprehensive risk assessment, it is necessary to choose the appropriate risk analysis method considering the actual scene requirements, the ability of analysts and other factors.

2.3 Approaches of Public Health Risk Identification for Emerging Infectious Diseases

2.3.1 Definition of Public Health Risk Identification for Emerging Infectious Diseases

Public health risk identification of emerging infectious diseases refers to the process of discovering, discriminating and describing public health risks caused by emerging infectious diseases, which is generally carried out around the "key issues" to be solved in the process of public health risk assessment caused by emerging infectious diseases. This includes both the identification of public health risk events, sources, causes and potential consequences of emerging infectious diseases, as well as the assessment of response capacity. Ways to identify risks include historical data analysis, theoretical analysis, informed opinion, expert opinion, and the multidimensional needs of stakeholders (Zhu and Shen 2017).

2.3.2 *Process of Public Health Risk Identification for Emerging Infectious Diseases (Xu and Wang 2017; Wu et al. 2014; Tong 2015)*

2.3.2.1 Data Collection and Analysis

The risk identification process in the public health risk assessment of emerging infectious diseases focuses on collecting and sorting out the risk factors related to the assessed infectious diseases, including the overview of infectious disease events, pathogen characteristics, clinical manifestations, epidemic characteristics, key links in the transmission process (sources of infection, transmission routes and susceptible persons), influencing factors in the epidemic process (natural and social factors), prevention and control measures, etc. (He and Wang 2016). In addition, if the disease is transmitted to humans by viruses or bacteria carried by animals, whether it will form a large scale of human-to-human transmission is also a key concern.

Overview and Background of Emerging Infectious Diseases

Information includes the time, place and population distribution of emerging infectious diseases; Local natural environment and social, economic and cultural factors related to the epidemic; Suspected contamination of drinking water and food; Whether there were special circumstances in the area around the time of the incident, such as large gatherings or events, natural disasters; Public or media attention, etc. The collection and collation of the above information will help to quickly understand the general picture and environmental conditions of emerging infectious diseases.

Relevant Characteristics of Emerging Infectious Diseases

A. Clinical manifestations of emerging infectious diseases. Including clinical symptoms, physical symptoms and clinical examination characteristics.
B. The pathogen category (viruses, bacteria, fungi, parasites, etc.), characteristics and the existing detection methods.
C. The reservoir conditions. A host that acts as a source of infection or plays a key role in transmission.

D. Mode of transmission. Describe the process of pathogen transmission, that is, whether the pathogen is transmitted by respiratory tract, intestinal transmission, insect-borne transmission, sexual transmission or blood transmission. If possible, quantify its propagation capacity, such as the basic regeneration number R_0.
E. Susceptible population. Identify which groups are susceptible. For vaccine-preventable infectious diseases, the level of immunization of the target population needs to be identified.
F. Incubation period. Includes the longest, shortest and average (or median) incubation periods of the disease.
G. Infectious period. For infectious diseases that can be transmitted directly from person to person, the transmission period needs to be identified.
H. Epidemiology. Three distribution characteristics of the disease, including the the season, area, population and extent, data sources including previous related literature and summarize
I. The incidence rate, mortality rate, and severe disease rate (hospitalization rate) of infectious diseases.
J. The control measures. Current preventive measures for healthy people: control measures for sick people, close contacts and contaminated environments, as well as in the event of an outbreak or epidemic.

Collect, sort out the above information will help to further understand the new process of the spread of infectious diseases and epidemic process, provide the basis for further identify and eliminate the risk.

Overview of Local Disease Prevalence

The surveillance data of infectious diseases in the incident area and related areas in recent years were analyzed to grasp the epidemic situation of the local disease. In most cases, however, this information is missing for emerging infectious diseases, especially those that are new or are not being monitored because they are not notifiable. In addition, the diagnosis of related cases in an emerging infectious disease emergency may not be accurate in medical institutions, and simple symptom descriptions are often used as diagnostic information in clinical practice, such as "viral meningitis" cases may be more diagnosed as "fever", "headache", "vomiting" and so on. In view of this, to reveal the epidemic dynamics as much as possible, non-traditional monitoring data sources can be fully mined to reveal the epidemic of infectious diseases, such as HIS data of medical institutions and school absence information.

Local Disease Response Capacity

The response capacity for emerging infectious disease emergencies includes: monitoring capacity, that is, the development of testing projects related to the disease in hospitals and CDC, and daily specimen testing; diagnosis and treatment capacity, that is, the medical resources and capacity that can undertake the related treatment tasks of the disease; the implementation of prevention and control measures, that is, daily prevention and control of the disease and emergency measures.

Data collection for risk identification can be realized through the following methods:

A. The system retrieval, screening literature, by systematic review target infectious disease related knowledge of historical literature, refining the best evidence;
B. On the basis of existing data extraction, analysis and monitoring;
C. Specifically for interview or expert advice.

2.3.2.2 Evidence Extraction and Evaluation

Due to different collectors and sources, the data used in the risk identification process is complicated and needs to be further summarized and refined before it can be used directly as supporting evidence for risk assessment. The extraction of evidence is generally based on the key questions raised in the previous stage, and lists its consideration factors, possible answers, answer basis, evidence sources, evidence quality, evidence uncertainty and other contents for each key question in the form of tables.

2.4 Approaches of Public Health Risk Analysis for Emerging Infectious Diseases

Based on risk identification, public health risk analysis of emerging infectious diseases is to understand the possibility of risk occurrence, estimate the consequences of risk, clarify the risk response ability, etc., by organizing expert consultation and other methods, and finally summarize the risk attributes of emerging infectious diseases and determine the risk level. Risk analysis generally includes the possibility of risk occurrence, the consequences caused or likely to be caused by risk, and the society's tolerance and control of risk (Xu and Wang 2017; Wu et al. 2014).

2.4.1 The Likelihood of Emerging Infectious Disease Events

In the process of public health risk assessment of emerging infectious diseases, "event occurrence" (and related events) is the fact resulting in the health damage and socio-economic impact of the population, which can be understood differently in different application contexts, including the import of emerging infectious diseases, infectious disease outbreaks, epidemic or high incidence of infectious diseases, high case fatality rate of infectious diseases and other states. The judgment of the "possibility" of an event comes from the description of all aspects of the characteristics, epidemic status and prevention and control measures of the disease in the process of risk identification.

The analysis of the risk of emerging infectious disease events should pay comprehensive attention to the etiology, clinical and epidemiological characteristics of the disease, the three elements of pathogen, environment and host, as well as the three steps of infection source, transmission route and susceptible persons, and should be combined with the event background, various monitoring information, historical events and hazards. The analysis of the possibility of emerging infectious diseases can establish the corresponding frequency risk factor and vulnerability factor index system, and qualitatively analyze the possibility of risk occurrence. It can also give the weight of each indicator for quantitative analysis. It is often difficult to establish the index system and set the weight for risk analysis of emerging infectious diseases. It is generally based on existing research, expert experience and knowledge. Table 2.1 gives the general framework of the "possibility" of emerging infectious disease events. Since there may be great differences in the index system and weights constructed for the same event, it is difficult to follow the unified standard to achieve high accuracy. In practice, personalized risk analysis should be carried out by combining the epidemic background of emerging infectious diseases, specific population and environment information.

The analysis of the possibility of an event cannot be simply based on theoretical knowledge, it should refer to work practice or actual situation, or even some empirical cognition. Such as considering whether there are local conditions and specific risk factors for the occurrence of a certain type of infectious disease, whether such events have occurred in the past, and whether such events have occurred in the surrounding area and caused harm. If there are similar events for reference, it can be confirmed with theoretical knowledge and strengthen the evidence for risk analysis.

2.4.2 The Severity of the Hams of Emerging Infectious Disease Emergencies

Analysis for the "severity" of the risk of an emerging infectious disease emergency requires attention not only to the harm to the health of the population, but also to its social impact. The population health hazards caused by infectious diseases can be measured by such indicators as morbidity, mortality, hospitalization rate, chronic or sequelae rate, duration of disease and severity of symptoms. The social impact caused by infectious diseases can be started from the two aspects of social stability and economic development, among which social stability can be manifested as the destruction of social life and production order and the impact of government credibility, etc., while the impact of economic development can be manifested as the

Table 2.1 Classification of the likelihood of emerging infectious diseases

Possibility of occurrence	Level	Identification of index	Take the possibility of importing dengue fever from abroad as an example
Almost certain to happen	5	Events occur under normal circumstances; It happens every year; Outbreaks or epidemics in surrounding areas; Serious increase in risk factors; Expert experience judgment, etc	The epidemic is serious overseas, the number of people entering country is increased (+ +), and the importation of cases is common under normal conditions
Likely to happen	4	Events can occur under most circumstances; Has occurred several times in the last 10 years, and has occurred at least once in the last 5 years; International, domestic and regional occurrence; The surrounding epidemic is severe; Increased risk factors; Expert experience judgment, etc	The epidemic is serious overseas, and the number of international travelers is increased
May happen	3	Events may occur in some circumstances; It happens every 10 years or more than once in 10 years and has happened in history; There are outbreaks in the surrounding areas; Risk factors exist; Expert experience judgment, etc	The epidemic is serious overseas, and the number of international travelers is moderate (+). Or the epidemic is moderate overseas, and the number of international travelers is increased (+ +)
Unlikely to happen	2	Events occurs on rare occasions; Unlikely to happen in 10 years; Low risk factors; Expert experience judgment, etc	The epidemic is moderate overseas, and the number of international travelers is rare (±)
Almost impossible to happen	1	Events may occur in rare circumstances; It has never happened or is considered unlikely to happen on the basis of reasonable knowledge; Risk factors are very low or non-existent	The disease is sporadic overseas, and the number of international travelers is rare (±)

cost of diagnosis and treatment (direct cost and indirect cost), and the economic loss caused by the damage of social production.

Specifically, analysis to the severity of the emerging infectious diseases occurrence includes the following elements:

A. The geographical extent of the spread of the disease and the number of people affected.
B. The number of cases and (or) the number of deaths and disability. Relevant statistical indicators include morbidity, recurrence rate, mortality rate, disability rate, etc.

C. The properties of unusual or unexpected events. For example, infectious diseases are caused by unknown factors, or their source, transmission, control measures are not clear; Previous prevention and control measures are poor effect or ineffective; Events develop more severely than expected, or symptoms are rare; Regional, seasonal or population distribution of the event are abnormal; The disease or factor causing the incident has been eliminated, eradicated within country, or has never been reported or occurred before.
D. There is a risk of widespread spread across regions, for example, where there is evidence of epidemiological links between the event and similar events in other regions; The incident occurred in a large gathering area, which may cause cross-regional transmission; The indicator case has a history of travel to multiple regions; Incidents caused by environmental pollution, etc., may spread across regions.
E. The diseases could have major public health impact, for example, high infectivity, high case fatality rate; There are no effective prevention and control measures; Events occur in special groups, such as children, older adults, people with low immunity or people with malnutrition, etc.; Events occur in special periods, such as major activities, major natural disasters, accidents and disasters; Events occurr in a densely populated area; Pathogens can spread widely, such as contaminated marketable food and drinking water.
F. Events may generate larger social impact. For instance, events have or may cause the relevant government departments concerned; Events have or may cause public concern; Events have or may attract media attention.

To analyze the severity of the risk of emerging infectious diseases, relevant sections can consider potential cause in advance, list the judgment standard. Table 2.2 can be used as a reference for evaluating the severity of emerging infectious disease events.

2.4.3 Risk Tolerance and Risk Control Ability

Risk tolerance for emerging infectious disease events refers to the objective capacity of individuals, organizations and governments to bear, which has been considered in the analysis of the possibility of emerging infectious disease emergencies or the severity of consequences. Additionally, it is also necessary to focus on the cognitive and psychological capacity of individuals, organizations and governments to bear the risk of emerging infectious disease events.

Risk control ability for emerging infectious diseases event mainly includes whether have experience dealing with similar incidents or risk, whether there is a series of diagnosis and treatment capacity, whether effective prevention and control measures are available, whether there is a complete responding organization and mechanism, whether there are sufficient resources available (e.g. manpower, preventive drugs and vaccines).

Table 2.2 Hazard severity classification of emerging infectious disease events

Severity of hazard	Level	Identification of index	Take the severity of the risk of importing and spreading dengue fever from abroad as an example
Severity	5	Severe symptoms and high mortality; occurrence of outbreak or epidemic; poor effect of control measures; unknown cause; causing huge economic losses and serious social impact; global attention, etc	Low level of medical institutions, no treatment experience (-); no effective monitoring system; poor effect of control measures; great social impact
Major	4	The proportion of severe disease is higher and the fatality rate is higher. The outbreak occurs and represents a tendency of secondary occurrence; Can cause certain economic losses and greater social impact; Have political or international sensitivity, etc	Great social impact; Medical institutions have little experience in treatment (±). The effect of monitoring is moderate. Control effect is unknown
Medium	3	Severe cases were common and the fatality rate was moderate. Outbreaks occur and persist for a period; The public is more concerned; Increased economic losses; Cause certain social influence and international influence	The level of medical institutions is high, and the treatment experience is moderate (+); Effective monitoring system: implementation of control measures; Great social impact
Not-significant	2	There are occasionally severe cases with low mortality. Scale of events is small, and the disease transmission path is limited. The ability to control spread is strong. Events will not cause economic losses. The public attention is low, and the social impact is small	High level of medical institutions and sufficient experience (+ +), or moderate experience but workers are recently trained. Perfect monitoring system; Effective control measures; Medium social influence
Minor	1	The symptoms are mild and death is rare; The scope of the event is limited; Strong control ability; The economic loss is small; Social impact is light	High level of medical institutions, rich experience of treatment (+ +), and preparing recent special training; Perfect monitoring system; Effective control measures; Low social impact

When the event risk is certain, and the risk tolerance and control ability are high, indicating it that corresponding "risk" is low. In most cases, the indicators related to risk tolerance and control ability cross and influence each other with the indicators of "possibility" and "severity" of disease occurrence, so "risk tolerance and control ability" is rarely analyzed independently. Common risk analysis methods include risk analysis flow chart method and risk matrix method. The former is mainly a list of factors such as the transmission link of emerging infectious diseases, disease consequences and control effects, and makes a "yes" or "no" judgment for each element according to evidence. It is a single algorithm that combines probability and influencing factors (Table 2.4). The latter evaluates three aspects: the possibility of spreading an emerging infectious disease within the local region, the possibility of spreading between different regions, and the impact after occurrence. Unlike the risk flow chart method, the risk matrix method calculates the probability and impact of the event risk separately (Table 2.5).

2.5 Approaches of Public Health Risk Evaluation for Emerging Infectious Diseases

On the basis of risk analysis, risk assessment relies on rigorous logic to organically combine the elements of risk analysis and the results obtained, balance the differences in the results of different aspects of risk analysis, and finally arrive at an overall impression that can reflect the assessment of the risk of emerging infectious diseases (Wu et al. 2014). The results of risk analysis are compared with risk criteria to determine the risk level of emerging infectious disease events.

The final result of risk assessment needs to be objective, accurate and repeatable. The objectivity and accuracy of risk assessment results are mainly reflected in the comprehensiveness and representation of risk elements included in the design of risk assessment methods (risk matrix, risk flow chart, etc.). Necessary risk elements should be considered as much as possible, and key points should be grasped, and some non-characteristic elements should be discarded when necessary. According to the types of risk factors of different emerging infectious diseases, the use of appropriate risk assessment tools will help to increase the accuracy and reliability of risk assessment. The repeatability of risk assessment results mainly depends on the accuracy and logical rigor of the understanding of components, in which each risk element must be clearly defined, and different assessors should have similar understanding without ambiguity. The organic combination or process of risk elements must conform to professional understanding and have strict logic.

Using the risk flow chart method (Table 2.3) to collect information, the risk level of emerging infectious disease events can be obtained through flow chart Fig. 2.3. If risk matrix method (Table 2.4) is used to collect problem evidence, flow charts Figs. 2.4 and 2.5 should be used to obtain the occurrence probability and consequences of emerging infectious disease events, and finally the risk level of the event can be obtained by combining the risk matrix table (Table 2.5).

Table 2.3 A flowchart method for risk analysis of emerging infectious disease emergencies

Problem/factor	Factor considered
1. Are there particular groups at high risk of infection? Yes/No	• Direct risk (like occupational) • Indirect risk (like Recipients of blood transfusions) • Population with special risk (like pregnant women, children)
2. How likely is the disease to spread within the local area? High/Low	Mode of transmission, incubation period, infection period, reproduction rate, susceptible population, etc. If it is a vector-borne disease, the vector density should also be considered The high risk for potential transmission including performance of strong infectivity and potential concentrated outbreak
3. Is the threat unusual or unexpected? Yes/No	Unusual diseases, environments, populations affected, increases in diseases beyond critical thresholds, emergence of previously unreported diseases
4. How likely is the disease to spread between regions? High/Low	The infectivity of the disease, the route of transmission, the susceptible population and the size of the population
5. Is this disease likely to cause serious illness in a population/group? Yes/No	Morbidity, mortality, case fatality rate, complications and burden of disease
6. Are there effective treatments and controls? Yes/No	Whether there are effective treatment methods, preventive measures and related materials
7. Are there relevant situational factors that might affect the risk assessment? Yes/No	Public understanding of risk, media interest, political/economic factors, special situations (e.g. major events, tourism, etc.)

Table 2.4 Risk matrix method for risk analysis of emerging infectious disease emergencies

Problem/factor	Factor considered
1. Are there particular groups at high risk of infection? Yes/No	• Direct risk (like occupational) • Indirect risk (like Recipients of blood transfusions) • Population with special risk (like pregnant women, children)
Probability of transmission of an infectious disease within region (Possibility of transmission)	
2. Is it possible that more people will be exposed? Yes/No	Mode of transmission, incubation period, period of infection, etc
3. Is the population highly susceptible? Yes/No	Number of susceptible people, immune status, number of possible cases
4. Is this infectious disease highly contagious? Yes/No	Factors related to the infectivity and transmissibility of the disease (such as mode of transmission, period of infection, and reproductive rate)
The probability of an infectious disease spreading between different regions (Possibility of transmission)	
5. Are there ways to import/spread to other areas? Yes/No	Infectivity and transmissibility of infectious diseases, route of importation/spread, number of susceptible populations and likely number of cases
6. Are people in other areas likely to be exposed? Yes/No	Infectivity and transmissibility of infectious diseases, route of importation/spread, number of susceptible populations and likely number of cases
7. Are people in other areas highly susceptible? Yes/No	The number of susceptible people and the number of potential cases
8. Is this infectious disease highly contagious? Yes/No	Factors related to the infectivity and transmissibility of the disease (such as mode of transmission, period of infection, and reproductive rate)
Effect of disease	
9. Does the disease cause serious illness in the population? Yes/No	Morbidity, mortality, case fatality rate, complications and burden of disease
10. Will large numbers of people be infected? Yes/No	Specific high-risk groups, direct and indirect risks, mode of transmission, reproductive rate, number of susceptible people and number of potential cases
11. Are there effective treatments and controls? Yes/No	Whether there are effective treatment methods, preventive measures and related materials
12. Are there relevant situational factors that might affect the risk assessment? Yes/No	Public understanding of risk, media interest, political/economic factors, special situations (e.g. major events, tourism, etc.)

Table 2.5 Risk matrix ranking table

Effect probability	Very low	Low	Medium	High
Very low	Very low risk	Low risk	Low risk	Medium risk
Low	Low risk	Low risk	Medium risk	Medium risk
Medium	Low risk	Medium risk	Medium risk	High risk
High	Medium risk	Medium risk	High risk	High risk
Very high	Medium risk	High risk	High risk	Very high risk

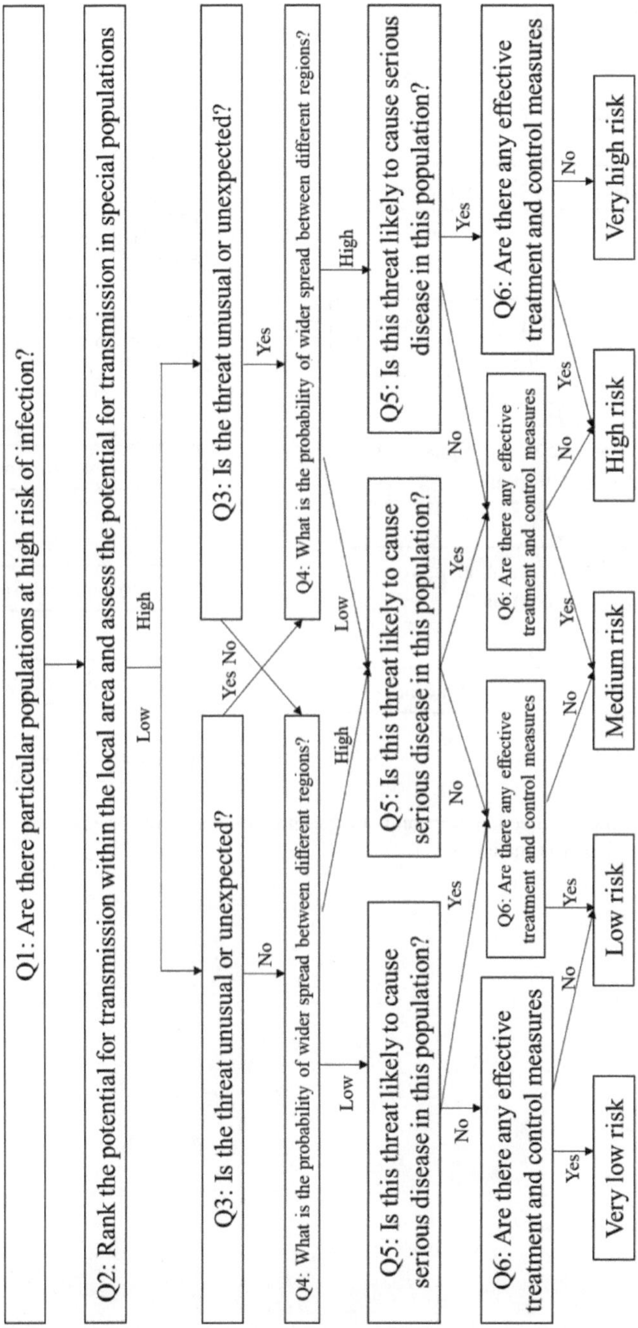

Fig. 2.3 Risk level determination based on risk flow chart method

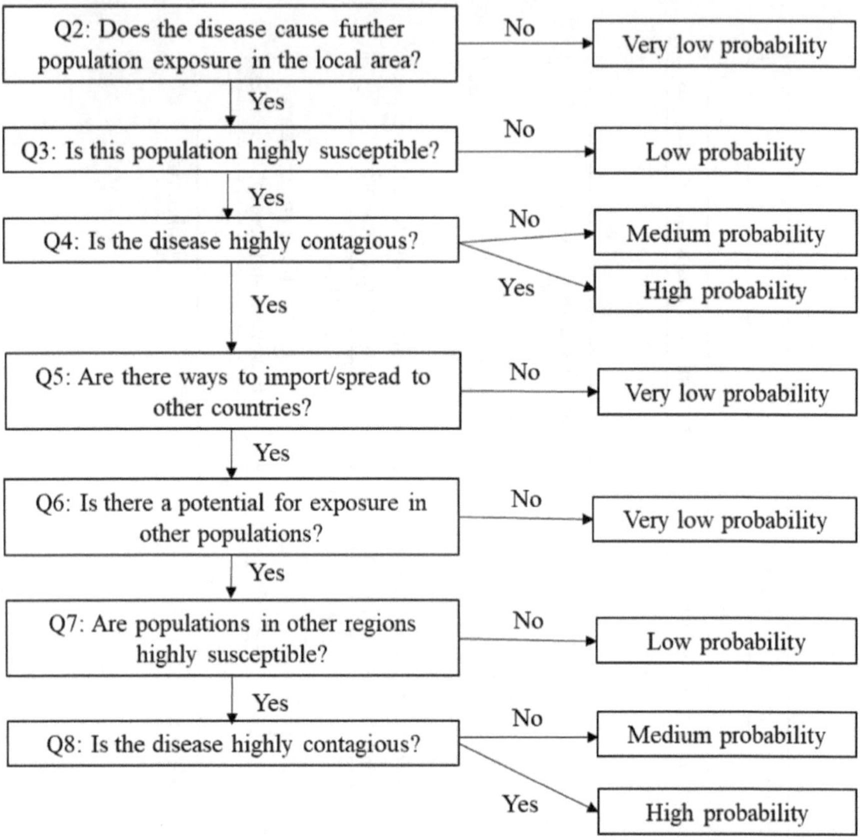

Fig. 2.4 Determination of infection probability or transmission possibility of emerging infectious diseases based on risk matrix method

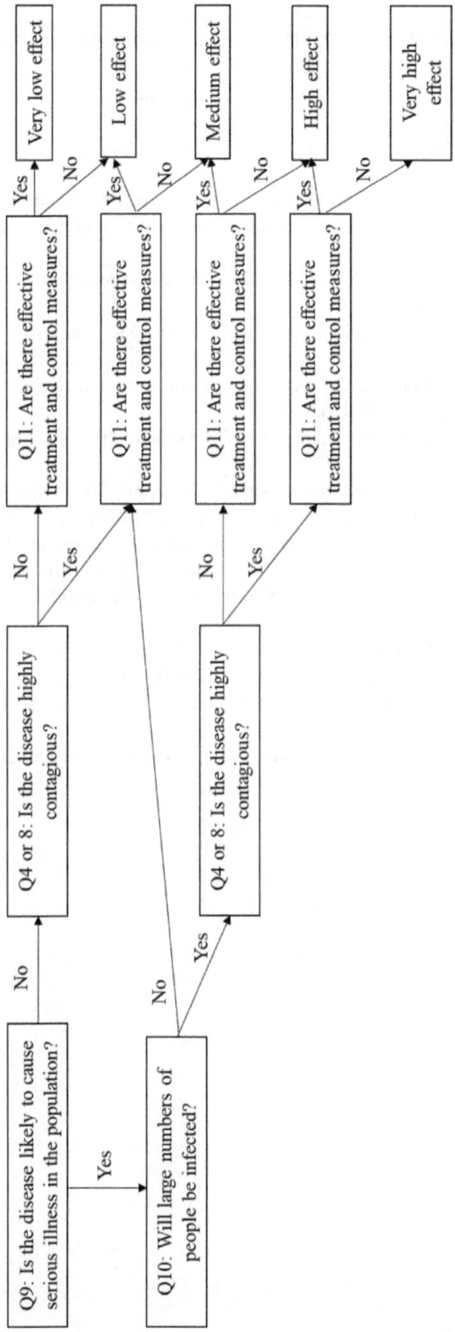

Fig. 2.5 Effect rating of emerging infectious diseases based on risk matrix method

References

Haldane V, De Foo C, Abdalla SM et al (2021) Health systems resilience in managing the COVID-19 pandemic: lessons from 28 countries. Nat Med 27(6):964–980

He X, Wang Q (2016) Identification and control of key infectious diseases. Science Press, China Beijing

Jones KE, Patel NG, Levy MA et al (2008) Global trends in emerging infectious diseases. Nature 451(7181):990–993

Liu J, Liu M, Liang W (2023) The 'Triangle Model' theory for prevention and control of newly emerging infectious diseases: definition, characteristics, and experience in China. Glob Transit 5:137–140

Liu J (2023) Prevention and control of major infectious diseases: theory and practice. China Union Medical College Press, Beijing

Lu H, Liang X (2018) Emerging infectious diseases. People's Medical Publishing House, China Beijing

Mahon MB, Sack A, Aleuy OA et al (2024) A meta-analysis on global change drivers and the risk of infectious disease. Nature 629(8013):830–836

Tong R (2015) Risk management theory and practice. China Labor and Social Security Press, China Beijing

World Health Organization (2023) Global tuberculosis report 2023. Geneva: World Health Organization. https://www.who.int/publications/i/item/9789240083851 (accessed 7 May 2023).

World Health Organization (2024) Global hepatitis report 2024. Geneva: World Health Organization. https://www.who.int/publications/i/item/9789240091672 (accessed 9 May 2024)

World Health Organization (n.d.) HIV and AIDS. https://www.who.int/news-room/fact-sheets/detail/hiv-aids (accessed 9 May 2024).

Wu Q, Kang Z, Jiao M (2014) A theoretical and technical Guide to public health Emergency Risk Assessment. People's Medical Publishing House, China Beijing

Xu S, Wang Y (2017) Theory and practice of emergency public health risk assessment. People's Medical Publishing House, China Beijing

Zhu F, Shen X (2017) Public health emergency response: theory and practice. Southeast University Press, China Jiangsu

Chapter 3
Public Health Emergency Management System

A Public Health Emergency is an event that can cause harm to a person's health or to the health of a community. These events can happen at any time, anywhere and include: outbreaks, such as COVID-19, Zika, and flu; accidental releases of industrial chemicals that can harm people's lungs, skin, and overall health; Intentional acts with biological, chemical, radiological, or nuclear agents; natural disasters, such as tornadoes, floods, wildfires, and hurricanes (Centers for Disease Control and Prevention 2021). The consequences of public health emergencies can be devastating for the health and well-being of communities and societies, the resilience of health systems, the stability of national economies, and progress towards the Sustainable Development Goals. The number of emergencies with health consequences will increase in the foreseeable future as risk factors increase. These include climate change; environmental degradation; urbanization; migration and international travel; State fragility; terrorism; and the lasting effect of the coronavirus disease 2019 (COVID-19) pandemic on health, societal and economic systems (World Health Organization 2024). This would pose a serious threat to human society, and recent experience has highlighted the global risk of infectious disease outbreaks, demonstrating the need to build a more effective emergency response system on health security and pandemic preparedness.

Emergency management subjects carry out the whole process of intervention and response before, during and after the emergency, which requires a series of systematic institutional systems to ensure support, including emergency management-related laws, systems, mechanisms, rules and regulations, capabilities and technologies, environment, culture, etc. The evolution and activities of such an emergency management system determine the capacity and efficiency of a country or region in responding to emergencies.

J. Liu, *Risk Management in Public Health*, Innovation in Risk Analysis,
https://doi.org/10.1007/978-981-97-6826-4_3

3.1 Introduction to Public Health Emergency Management System

3.1.1 Public Health Emergency

Public health emergency refers to the sudden occurrence of major infectious disease outbreaks, unexplained diseases in groups, major food and occupational poisoning, and other events that seriously affect public health, causing or probably causing serious damage to public health in the society. There are various classifications of public health emergency, from the cause of occurrence, usually can be divided into: diseases caused by biological pathogens, food poisoning events, group poisoning caused by contamination of toxic and hazardous factors, the emergence of poisoning deaths or hazards, natural disasters: natural disasters, such as earthquakes, volcanic eruptions, mudslides, typhoons, floods, and other sudden attacks, accidental deaths, group illnesses or deaths caused by unknown reasons (Chinese Center for Disease Control and Prevention n.d.).

The International Health Regulations (IHR) (2005) issued by the World Health Organization (WHO) define a Public Health Emergency of International Concern (PHEIC) as: "an extraordinary event which is determined to constitute a public health risk to other States through the international spread of disease and to potentially require a coordinated international response". This definition implies a situation that is: serious, sudden, unusual or unexpected; carries implications for public health beyond the affected State's national border; and may require immediate international action (World Health Organization 2016). Each State Party shall assess and communicate events that may constitute PHEIC in accordance with the decision-making document shown in Fig. 3.1 (World Health Organization 2016). Since the establishment of this mechanism, the Director-General has identified PHEIC seven times: H1N1 in 2009, poliovirus in 2014, Ebola in 2014 and 2019, Zika in 2016, COVID-19 in 2020 and mpox in 2022 (Wenham and Stout 2024). Public health emergencies involve increased incidence of illness, injury and/or death and require special measures to address increased morbidity, mortality and interruption of essential health services. For such emergencies, a multi-agency, multi-jurisdictional response is often required, working with the national disaster management organization. When normal resources and capacities are exceeded, support from outside the affected areas will also be required. External assistance could include national, cross-border, regional or international resources (World Health Organization 2015).

3.1.2 Public Health Emergency Management System

The public health emergency management system refers to the sum of emergency response elements such as organizations, systems, behaviors, resources, and the relationship between the elements when responding to a public health emergency. The

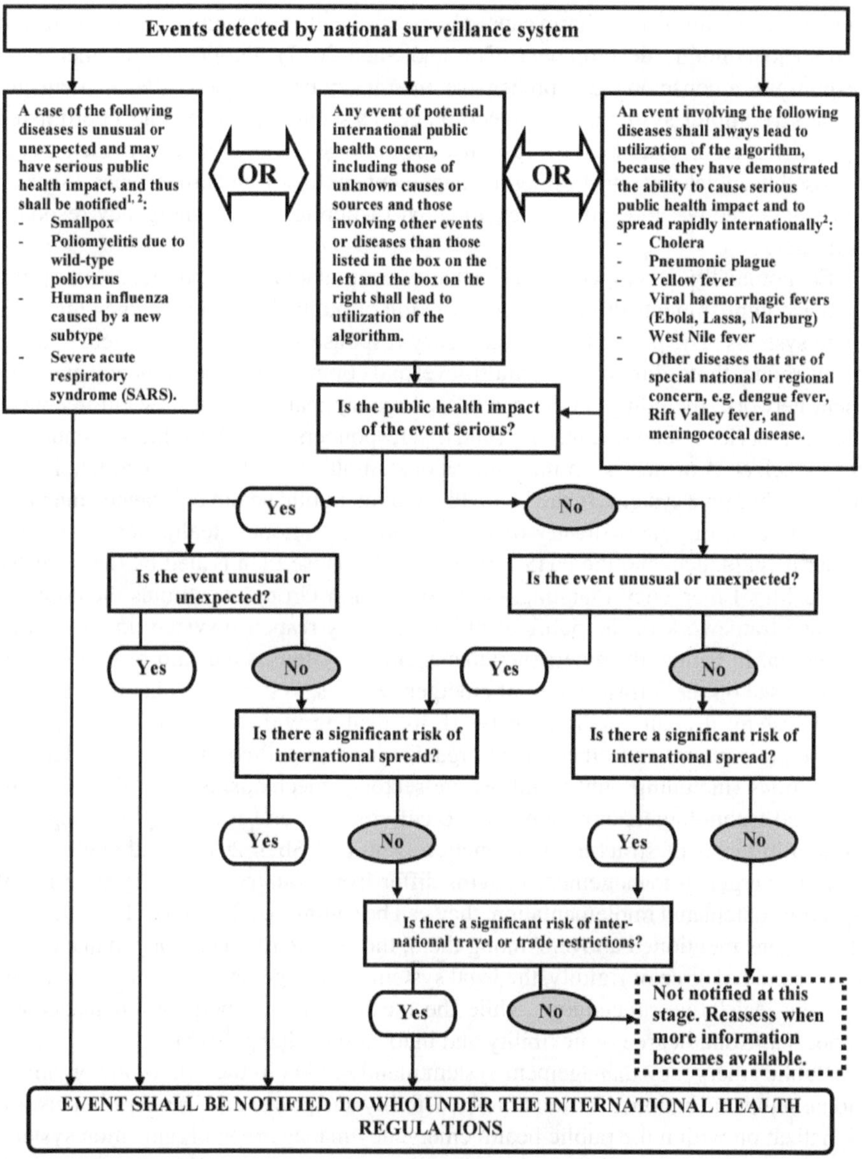

Fig. 3.1 Decision instruments for the assessment and notification of events that may constitute public health emergencies of international concern (*Note* [1]As per WHO case definitions; [2]The disease list shall be used only for the purposes of these Regulations)

purpose is to minimize the harm caused by public health emergencies to public health and socioeconomic development (Zhu and Shen 2017). Public health emergency response as a conscious, comprehensive emergency practice activities, its management is a complex systematic engineering, need a scientific, reasonable, coordinated operation system, to address the response to public health emergencies in the process of possible unclear responsibilities, management confusion and other issues, to maximize the effective and orderly development of public health emergency response activities.

Economically developed countries have accumulated rich experience and practical accomplishments during the construction of public health emergency management systems. The public health emergency response system of the United States is an all-round, three-dimensional, multi-level and comprehensive emergency management network, including public health, emergency management, law enforcement, medical services, scientific research and first responders (e.g., firefighters, ambulance personnel, etc.), which is a multi-dimensional, multi-disciplinary, integrated, linked and collaborative system. In the United Kingdom, public health emergency management is shared by the Ministry of Health and the National Health Service (NHS) under its guidance, and the NHS Emergency Response Plan issued by the Ministry of Health's Emergency Planning and Coordination Group constitutes the comprehensive framework of the public health emergency response system in the United Kingdom. In China, the emergency management system is the sum of four dimensions based on the infrastructure of emergency plans, systems, mechanisms and the legal system; it is an integrated network for dealing with emergencies constituted by the government and other social organizations, including laws and regulations, institutions (including public and private sectors), mechanisms and rules, capabilities and technologies, environment and culture, etc., and it is a highly integrated system in terms of structure and function (Zhu and Shen 2017). Although public health emergency management systems differ from country to country in terms of specific content and implementation, they can be summarized in general into the four dimensions mentioned above. Among them, the system of emergency management has a certain degree of rigidity, the legal system of emergency management requires specific legislative procedures, while the mechanism of emergency management reflects a strong degree of flexibility and innovation (Zhang 2016).

Public emergency management system mainly refers to the sum of the organizational setup, affiliation, division of responsibility and power and its operation institutionalization within the public health emergency management organization system. It is the main structure of the national management of public health emergencies, all emergency response work is to organize, implement and complete through this main structure, the rationality of its structure will be directly related to the results of the response to public health emergencies. The public health emergency management mechanism refers to the specific application process of the emergency management system and method, and the interaction between the elements, which is a complex work system. Emergency legal system refers to the laws, regulations and rules related to emergency management. The emergency plan system is an important part of the construction for public health emergency response, and is the cornerstone of the early warning and prediction capacity for emergencies, as well as the guarantee for improving the public health emergency response capacity (Zhang 2016).

3.2 Emergency Plan for Public Health Emergencies

Emergency plan is the possible occurrence of major events, accidents or disasters, in order to ensure rapid, efficient and orderly emergency response and rescue work, minimize losses and pre-established relevant programs or action plans. Emergency plan is the core of public emergency disposal, contains a wealth of past experience and knowledge of disposal, pre-defined event description of emergency disposal, emergency organizational structure, resources for response, as well as the process of emergency disposal provides for the start of the plan conditions (i.e., which type of which level of events), how to dispose of the principle (i.e., what kind of resources are needed, what roles to do, how to do) and the event disposal process. The establishment of a sound mechanism for handling emergency plans can enhance the ability and level of handling incidents. The emergency plan clearly defines the handling procedures and responsible subjects of each department and each link. Once an incident occurs, the emergency plan can be activated. Under the command and coordination of the commander, the relevant departments will actively and orderly carry out effective emergency response work.

Depending on the character of the emergency plan, it can be categorized as a strategic-level plan, an operational-level plan, a tactical-level plan and a field action plan. Strategic-level plan is located at the top level of the emergency plan system. Its main function is to provide policy guidance, overall layout, and put forward the vision and goals of national emergency management. Operational-level emergency plan is mainly based on specific scenarios of various disasters, describing the tasks and responsibilities of the government and departments in emergency management, as well as the mechanisms and procedures for unified coordination, and should be continuously improved based on the evaluation results of exercises and practices. Tactical-level emergency plan is generated on the basis of operational plan, and improved and perfected according to the random scenarios in the field, the main target is to participate in the field emergency response action of the functional units, such as responsible for or involved in the engineering rescue medical care and logistical support and other units. Tactical level emergency plan structure and content should have good flexibility and operability, the main development and users are government departments and their subordinate units. The field action plan focuses on random scenarios during an emergency event and applies only to a complete operation or a single task. The field action plan is generally formulated at the scene by the unit specifically tasked with emergency response responsibilities (e.g., medical ambulance team, fire suppression team, etc.) and is clear, explicit and specific about the time, location, personnel and activities of the emergency operation. These four types of emergency plans form the basic prototypes of the various types of functional plans (Zhu and Shen 2017).

The IHR (2005) indicates that the capacity for public health response at the national level requires the development, implementation and maintenance of national public health emergency plans, including the establishment of multidisciplinary and multisectoral working groups to respond to events that could constitute a PHEIC (World Health Organization 2016). The specific content of the emergency plan for public health emergency varies from country to country, but generally includes the following aspects: (1) Emergency command system: to clarify the composition of the emergency command organization of public health emergencies, responsibilities and division of labor. (2) Emergency responsibilities: to clarify the responsibilities and tasks of various departments and units in the emergency response to public health emergencies. (3) Emergency measures: to clarify the emergency response to public health emergencies, including monitoring, early warning, investigation, isolation, control, treatment, material security, maintenance of social order. (4) Emergency training: to clarify the organization, implementation and evaluation of emergency training. (5) Revision of emergency plan: to clarify the procedures and time limit for the revision of the emergency plan.

3.3 Public Health Emergency Management System

3.3.1 Framework for a Public Health Emergency Operations Centre of WHO (World Health Organization 2015)

The incident management system (IMS) is a common organizational model for all hazards and emergencies. The IMS outlines responsibilities for management, operations, planning, logistics, finance, administration, policy, and communications. It can be adapted to the context of the incident, to accommodate the interests and mandates of responding agencies with potentially overlapping authorities, responsibilities, and roles. The management function is an executive, strategic, operational, command and coordination function that involves making decisions and coordinating risk communication. The planning section is responsible for evaluation of the situation (information gathering and analysis), assessment of the options for dealing with it, and keeping track of resources. The operations section deals with supporting tactical application of resources. The logistics section deals with acquiring and deploying resources. The financial and administrative section tracks expenditure, makes payments, and provides administrative services. This five-function IMS model is flexible and can be adapted to individual events, agencies and jurisdictions, whether local, regional, or national, according to needs and available resources. The organizational structure for command and response is shown in Fig. 3.2.

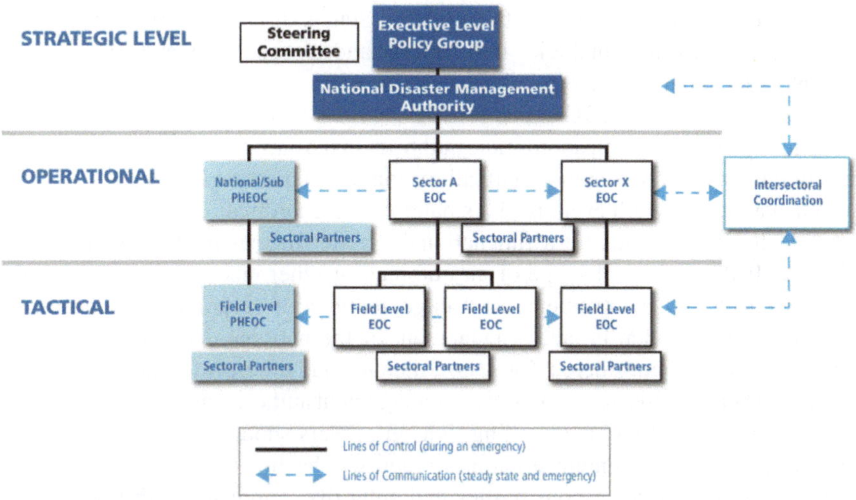

Fig. 3.2 Organizational structure for command and response

3.3.1.1 Strategic and Policy Level

This is the highest level of the national disaster management structure and is responsible for strategic coordination and policy making. It is usually led by the office of the president/prime minister or a cabinet level delegate, with executive management capacity from participating agencies. It may also include key technical partners and political representatives from the affected districts.

With regard to responsibilities and relevant actions, the strategic level: Provides high-level direction for the response; Determines the need to declare a national-level emergency; Determines when the state of national-level emergency has ended; Makes and endorses policy required to enable the response; Establishes national and multinational objectives; Develops national-level plans to support these objectives; Coordinates the response of national-level agencies; Monitors the operational coordination and implementation of the strategy; Ensures provision of human resources and other capabilities as needed to support operations and to achieve established objectives; and Prepares and/or approves public communications materials, technical guidance and activities.

In most countries and under a multi-hazard approach, this function is normally assigned to the national disaster management authorities such as the national disaster management office or a similar agency.

A ministry-level emergency operations center (EOC) should be established to coordinate planning and operations with other responding ministries and partners, and to control and coordinate the activities of operational-level EOCs for a public health response. This may include coordination with international partners to ensure strategic-level unity of effort. At the Member State's discretion, they may coordinate international efforts including international and non-governmental organizations through the UN cluster system.

In the absence of an EOC at this level, there must be adequate representation by the ministry of health, with appropriate authority in the national disaster management structure to ensure coordination with all responders at a strategic level.

When a public health event is of a smaller scale, coordination might be achieved through the EOC alone and a full national disaster management structure is not required. If the scale and scope of an outbreak or other emergency were to escalate, requiring the involvement of a large number of responders from outside the health agency, then broader engagement of the national disaster management authority should be considered. Close coordination and timely information exchange is required between the national disaster management authority and other responding agencies. When an EOC is operating, liaison officers should be maintained at the national disaster management structure to represent health issues.

To ensure clarity of responsibilities and authority, senior leadership within the national government must identify 'supported' and 'supporting' relationships among the response agencies. The supported agency is the agency with the responsibility, authority, and technical expertise to best manage the incident or event. Supporting agencies are those with additional or available resources, including personnel, material, and expertise, that the supported agency requires. When a supporting agency or jurisdiction is contributing.

3.3.1.2 Operational (Coordination) Level

The operational level is responsible for effective coordination of all response elements and maintenance of situational awareness for strategic-level authorities.

With regard to responsibilities and relevant actions, the operational level: Provides the technical lead for the operational response based on strategic guidance; Develops operational-level plans to meet strategic objectives; Coordinates the response of the agency with other responding agencies, including international partners responding at the operational level; Controls and maintains situational awareness of tactical units and their actions; Prioritizes and provides the resources to support response activities at the tactical level; and Provides the 'common operating picture' against which strategic and operational decisions are made.

In some settings, the operational and strategic-level responsibilities can be combined into a single EOC. In a resource-constrained environment, the operational-level EOC may reside at the national level.

Where there are other agencies maintaining EOCs, it is essential to coordinate operational level planning with these EOCs to ensure efficient use of resources and unity of effort. When possible, responding agencies, including international partners, should place a liaison officer within the operational-level EOC to maintain unity of effort.

3.3.1.3 Tactical (Implementation) Level

The third level of a response is the tactical management of response operations. Unlike the national or subnational levels, this will normally be located as close to the incident as possible, at district or community level. This may take the form of a mobile and temporary command post, an EOC staffed by all agencies responding locally, or a local public health-specific EOC.

This level is responsible for the day-to-day actions that will achieve the established strategic and operational goals and objectives. To accomplish these actions, the tactical EOC will generally develop incident action plans that focus on measurable and achievable actions by tactical resources during a set 'operational period' (typically 24 h for a public health response). Tactical planning within the incident action plan will describe what mechanisms will be used with the available resources to achieve the desired results.

Decisions related to tactical actions should be made at the lowest level possible.

The tactical level should have the freedom to determine a course of action based on assigned objectives. Higher levels should avoid directing specific actions or tasks except as dictated by policy or resource limitations. The tactical level should be able to reach up to the operational level to request resources as needed to complete assigned objectives.

As with the higher levels, coordination between the EOC and other agencies, including international partners, in the local response is crucial to ensuring the best outcomes.

3.3.1.4 Incident/event Grading and EOC Scaling

Grading refers to an assessment of the level of risk associated with an incident, considering such factors as its geographic extent, complexity, severity and duration, and the extent of existing internal and acquired external resources required to resolve it. The grading process—the risk assessment—starts immediately upon detection/notification or alert, to ensure that a response is appropriately urgent and adequately resourced. Continual reassessment of the incident is required to ensure necessary escalation or de-escalation.

The process is often triggered at a tactical level, but becomes operational and strategic as additional resources are required or pre-established thresholds are exceeded. A gradient of levels, often three to five in number, is based on the increasing level of response resources required, and triggers escalating levels or phases of EOC activation. The higher the grade of an incident, the more response and management resources will be required, and the more fully developed the EOC activation will need to be.

Upon alert that an incident with elevated risk has occurred or is imminent, the responsible agency (ministry of health if designated) appoints an incident manager to monitor the event and adjust the grading and the scale of the response as the situation evolves. In a national level EOC the highest grading, regardless of the number of grades, would be characterized by extensive impact on the population and the health system, and would require a coordinated, multi-sectoral, multi-jurisdictional response with international assistance.

3.3.2 *Examples of Public Health Emergency Management Systems in Different Countries*

3.3.2.1 China: "National-Provincial-City-County" Four- Level Vertical Management System

The public health emergency management in China is vertical, with the gradual establishment and improvement of a four-level organizational system of public health emergency management relations at the central, provincial, city (prefecture) and county levels (Fig. 3.3) (Zhu and Shen 2017; Zhang 2016).

The State Council is the highest administrative leading organization for public health emergency response. Under the leadership of the State Council, the National Health Commission makes decisions on whether to set up a national emergency response headquarters based on the seriousness of the public health emergency.

The national emergency command, which is composed of the military and relevant departments, is responsible for unifying the command in the event of a public health emergency, coordinating with the Health Commission, the Chinese Center for Disease Control and Prevention and other relevant departments to ensure that these

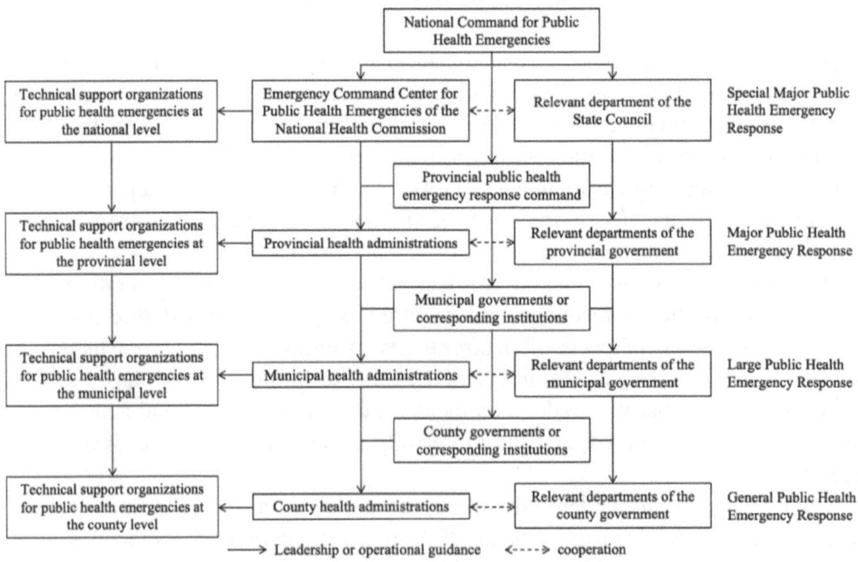

Fig. 3.3 Framework of public health emergency management system in China

departments are able to work together in a coordinated manner to respond to various emergencies, and at the same time, formulating emergency plans and overall plans, and promoting the construction of an emergency plan system and the rehearsal of such plans, in order to prevent and minimize the impact of public emergencies on society.

The National Health Commission undertakes health emergency and treatment work, leads lower-level organizations to handle public health incidents, informs the status of epidemics timely, and is the highest operational command body for emergency response.

Under the leadership of governments at all levels, the health departments of provinces, autonomous regions, and municipalities directly have set up corresponding emergency headquarters. The highest responsible person is generally the highest leader of the government of the region, and is responsible for the command of public health emergencies within the region. According to the needs of public health emergencies, mobilize personnel, materials and means of transport within the administrative region to participate in the emergency response, coordinate the emergency response work of medical aid agencies, the center for disease control and prevention and other relevant departments within the region, carry out mass prevention and control, maintain social stability, and formulate an overall response plan.

Municipal and county health departments, under the leadership of their governments, set up emergency response commands at the municipal and county levels, strictly adhere to the commands of higher authorities, actively implement policies issued by higher authorities, and assist higher authorities in the emergency response work in their regions.

3.3.2.2 United States: All-Round, Three-Dimensional, Multi-Level and Comprehensive Emergency Management Network (Mu et al. 2020)

The United States has explored the construction of a system for managing public health emergencies earlier. After experiencing the challenges of viral encephalitis in 1999, the "9·11" incident in 2001, anthrax in 2002, monkeypox virus in 2003, and the H1N1 virus in 2009, the United States has continued to build and improve the response system for public health emergencies in the course of dealing with each emergency, and has formed an all-round, three-dimensional, multilevel, and comprehensive emergency management network. Its comprehensiveness lies in the collaborative system of public health, emergency management, law enforcement, medical services, scientific research and first responders (e.g., firefighters, ambulance personnel). In 1979, the United States began to pilot Federal Emergency Management Agency as the core of a comprehensive emergency management model, that is, the adoption of the "federal-state-local" three-tier management system, is a vertical system as the main system, the horizontal system as the sub-system (Fig. 3.4).

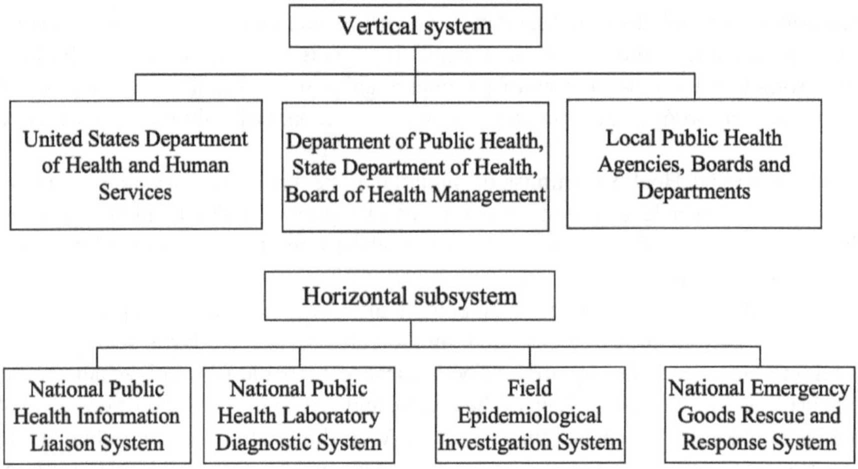

Fig. 3.4 Vertical and horizontal system for public health emergency response in the United States

The Centers for Disease Control and Prevention is part of the United States Department of Health and Human Services and plays a leading role in public health emergency response. Its main functions include the development of overall strategies for disease surveillance and control, mass population vaccination, epidemiological surveys, experimental research, etc.

State agencies, etc. in the vertical system have a great deal of autonomy within their jurisdictions and can be approached for help without being directly regulated by the federal government. Local departments and agencies are still given autonomy to respond to incidents and have territorial authority.

State and local governments, as first responders, build horizontal subsystems, upload information on time through the four horizontal subsystems for information sharing, joint diagnosis to improve the correctness rate, analyze the causes of the disease by carrying out epidemiological investigations, take preventive measures and stockpile and deploy emergency items. The operation of these inter-systems ensures the smooth running of the emergency response.

This United States emergency response system, which is primarily vertical and horizontally based, has greatly improved the efficiency of the United States in dealing with public health emergencies. In the event of a public health emergency, health care providers and other public sectors are able to work together in a coordinated manner to respond.

3.3.2.3 Canada: Three-Level Response System for the FPT

In Canada, emergency management consists of four interdependent components, including prevention and mitigation, preparedness, response, and recovery. These four interdependent components may be undertaken sequentially or concurrently, but they are not independent of each other. Emergency management in provincial, territorial and federal governments adopts a comprehensive all-hazards approach to coordinate and integrate prevention and mitigation, preparedness, response and recovery functions to maximize the safety of Canadians. Ensuring a strong and seamless relationship across these components and with appropriate emergency management partners, including Indigenous peoples and municipalities/communities, through mechanisms such as mutual aid agreements, is critical to effective emergency management (Ministers Responsible for Emergency Management 2017).

The public health emergency management system in Canada consists of three levels: Federal/Provincial/Territorial (FPT) (Ministers Responsible for Emergency Management 2017). FPT governments operate cooperatively within the jointly established FPT emergency management governance structure, which facilitates coordination and collaboration in full respect of each government's legislated jurisdiction. Figure 3.5 provides a summary overview of the FPT emergency management governance structure. It is based on three governing tiers and a variety of FPT co-chaired working groups that support agreed upon decisions and strategic directions.

FPT Ministers occupy the top tier in the FPT emergency management governance structure. FPT Deputy Ministers are the second tier of the structure, and are responsible for implementing ministerial decisions by setting priorities and assigning FPT Senior Officials Responsible for Emergency Management to take responsibility for action items. Working Groups report to the FPT Senior Officials Responsible for Emergency Management, submitting proposals and reporting on the results of their ongoing work. There is no reporting relationship between the FPT Senior Officials Responsible for Emergency Management and Canada's Platform for Disaster Risk Reduction Advisory Committee; however, the two groups work closely together to advance Disaster Risk Reduction and emergency management priorities.

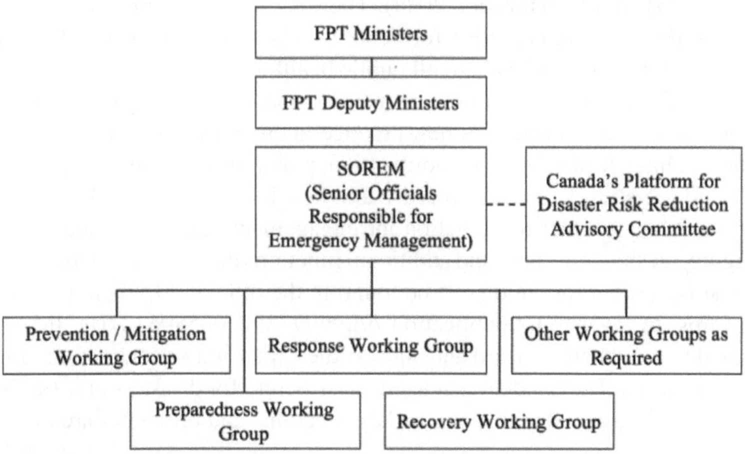

Fig. 3.5 FPT governance structure in Canada (*Note* The working groups identified in the above diagram may be stood-up or stood-down by SOREM as needed to address priorities)

The composition of the Working Groups is based on the multi-sectoral nature of emergency management and may require the participation of FPT government partners from different departments. There are four standing Working Groups that are organized according to the four components of emergency management. There are additional horizontal Working Groups, and sub-working groups that also report to Senior Officials Responsible for Emergency Management (SOREM), which are created and operate as required.

The Ministerial tier of the governance structure oversees the Deputy Ministers' tier, which in turn oversees the Senior Officials Responsible for Emergency Management. The Senior Officials Responsible for Emergency Management in turn oversees the various Working Groups and then report up the governance structure on progress.

Regular meetings and teleconferences support the ongoing operations of the entire FPT governance structure. Working Groups hold meetings and teleconferences as required based on workload and timelines, while respecting the schedule of other tiers of the FPT emergency management governance structure.

The FPT emergency management governance structure, its Working Groups and the guidelines set out in the Framework has led, among other things, to the creation of FPT emergency management strategies and concordant action plans for their implementation.

3.4 Public Health Emergency Management Mechanism

Developed by the WHO, the Emergency Response Framework (ERF) is internal WHO guidance on how the Organization manages the assessment of, grading of, and response to public health events in support of Member States and affected communities (World Health Organization 2024). The ERF focuses primarily on scaling up and managing response activities for acute events and emergencies. It adopts an all-hazards approach, applicable to all public health events and emergencies. In this framework, WHO's response to emergencies is managed through the IMS, which is internationally recognized as a best practice in emergency management. Its core functions include: leadership and coordination, planning and monitoring, operations support and logistics, technical expertise and health operations, health information and epidemiology, partner coordination and engagement, and finance and administration. Figure 3.6 shows the core and additional functions of the IMS and its operational mechanisms; more information can be found in the official document published by WHO (https://www.who.int/publications/i/item/9789240058064). The IMS should be adapted to the specific hazard and address the expansion or contraction of service and support needs. The incident management structure for disasters may be different from that for disease outbreaks, but the key functions and principles are the same.

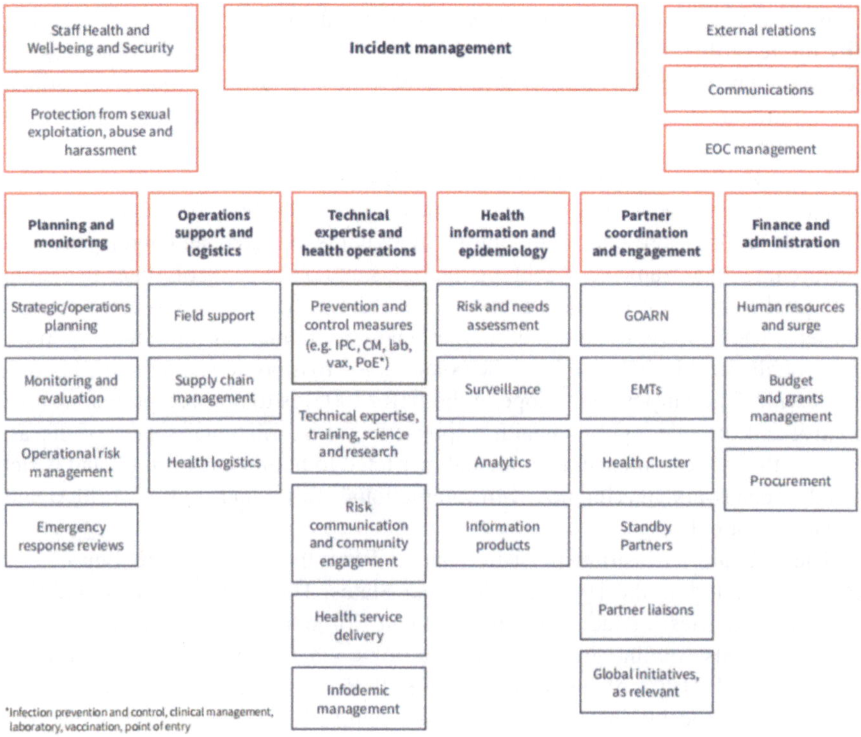

Fig. 3.6 Functions and mechanisms of the public health emergency management

3.5 Public Health Emergency Management Legal System

The Public Health Emergency Management Legal System (PHEMLS) is a general term for the laws, regulations, rules and policy norms formulated for the prevention, control and disposal of public health emergencies. It is an important part of the global, national and regional governance system, and is a legal guarantee for the maintenance of global public health security.

In order to effectively respond to public health emergencies, the establishment of a sound PHEMLS is essential. On the one hand, human society is faced with the threat of sudden natural disasters, accidental disasters, public health emergencies and social security incidents. The legalization of public health emergency management is conducive to the creation of a legally supportive environment for the response to public health emergencies, and ensures the legitimacy and effectiveness of the response measures, so as to achieve effective prevention and control of public health emergencies and minimize the cost of national and social crises. On the other hand, it is an inevitable trend in the twenty-first century for the national and international community to establish a legal system for responding to public health emergencies, so as to safeguard public health by means of national coercive force and internationally unified rules, and to promote the harmonious development of the society and economy. The PHEMLS consists of four levels of laws and regulations: international laws, national laws, local laws and regulations, as well as rules and regulations, and policy norms.

International law is the foundation of PHEMLS and consists mainly of international treaties and normative documents such as the IHR (2005) developed by WHO. The IHR (2005) represents a binding international legal agreement and provides an overarching legal framework defining the rights and obligations of States in dealing with public health events and emergencies that have the potential to cross national borders. Their aim is to help the international community prevent and respond to acute public health risks that have the potential to cross borders and threaten people worldwide. The purpose and scope of the IHR (2005) is to prevent, protect against, control and provide a public health response to the international spread of disease in ways that are commensurate with and restricted to public health risks, and which avoid unnecessary interference with international traffic and trade (World Health Organization n.d).

The IHR are an instrument of international law that is legally-binding on 196 countries, including the 194 WHO Member States. They create rights and obligations for countries, including the requirement to report public health events. The Regulations also outline the criteria to determine whether or not a particular event constitutes a PHEIC. At the same time, the IHR require countries to designate a National IHR Focal Point for communications with WHO, to establish and maintain core capacities for surveillance and response, including at designated points of entry. Additional provisions address the areas of international travel and transport such as the health documents required for international traffic. Finally, the IHR introduce important safeguards to protect the rights of travelers and other persons in relation to the treatment of personal data, informed consent and non-discrimination in the application of health measures under the Regulations (World Health Organization 2016; World Health Organization n.d.).

The responsibility for implementing the IHR rests upon all States Parties that are bound by the Regulations and on WHO. Governments are responsible, including all of their sectors, ministries, levels, officials and personnel for implementing IHR at the national level. WHO plays the coordinating role in IHR implementation and, together with its partners, helps countries to build capacities. The IHR require that all countries have the ability to do the following: (1) Detect: Make sure surveillance systems can detect acute public health events in timely matter; (2) Assess and report: Use the decision instrument in Annex 2 of the IHR to assess public health event and report to WHO through their National IHR Focal Point those that may constitute a PHEIC; (3) Respond: Respond to public health risks and emergencies. The goal of country implementation is to limit the spread of health risks to neighboring countries and to prevent unwarranted travel and trade restrictions (World Health Organization 2016; World Health Organization n.d.).

In order to respond effectively to public health emergencies, each country and region has established a corresponding legal system. The system consists of constitutions and laws, administrative regulations, local laws and regulations, rules and other normative documents, and usually stipulates the duties and powers of the government in public health emergencies, as well as the rights and obligations of citizens.

In Australia, for example, the emergency legal system is hierarchical, with laws at different levels of government to enable effective cooperation between organizations and governments (Zhou 2020). At the Commonwealth level, the Quarantine Act was established in 1908 to prevent the introduction and spread of specific diseases within Australia. At the Commonwealth level, the Quarantine Act was established in 1908 to prevent the introduction and spread of specific diseases within Australia. The Disaster Management Act was enacted in 2003 to provide a mechanism for States and other agencies to respond, coordinate and cooperate in responding to disasters... The National Health Security Act was enacted in 2007 to specify requirements for the implementation of public health surveillance. In addition, the Australian Crisis Management Act sets out the duties, powers and procedures of the government in responding to emergencies. At the local level, states (territories) have also formulated independent statutes and regulations to effectively respond to emergencies, such as the New South Wales Emergency and Rescue Management Act enacted by the State of New South Wales in 1989 and the Queensland Disaster Management Act enacted by the State of Queensland in 2003. To better enable effective cooperation between federal and local governments, Australia has also introduced the National Health Security Agreement, which supports the National Health Security Act issued by the federal Government and sets out the framework for national decision-making responses to health emergencies.

In order to ensure the effective operation of the public health emergency management system, the United States has also established a relatively complete legal system for responding to public health emergencies, and in 1988 introduced the Stafford Disaster Mitigation and Emergency Assistance Act, which is used to guide disaster relief and mitigation efforts. In terms of responding to public health emergencies, a federal law, the Public Health Service Act, was passed in 1994, which has clear provisions on the definition of serious infectious diseases, the formulation of regulations for controlling infectious diseases, the duties of quarantine officials, etc. In addition, the United States law gives states a high degree of autonomy. States and counties have also formulated laws and regulations to prevent the spread of infectious diseases, which provide strong legal safeguards for dealing with emerging infectious diseases (Zhou 2020).

In conclusion, the public health emergency management legal system is an important legal guarantee for the maintenance of national public health security. By improving the public health emergency management legal system, we can effectively improve the prevention and control ability of public health emergencies and the level of emergency response, and effectively safeguard the lives and health of the public.

References

Centers for Disease Control and Prevention (2021) About the Office of Readiness and Response. https://www.cdc.gov/orr/aboutus/index.htm (accessed 16 April 2024).

Chinese Center for Disease Control and Prevention (n.d.) Public Health Emergency. https://www.chinacdc.cn/jkzt/tfggwssj/ (accessed 22 April 2024).

Ministers Responsible For Emergency Management (2017) An emergency management framework for Canada - Third Edition. https://www.publicsafety.gc.ca/cnt/rsrcs/pblctns/2017-mrgnc-mngmnt-frmwrk/index-en.aspx (accessed May 2 2024).

Mu L, Lu X, Zhao L (2020) Comparison of public health emergency management systems in China and abroad. Financial Management Research 4:65–73

Wenham C, Stout L (2024) A legal mapping of 48 WHO member states' inclusion of public health emergency of international concern, pandemic, and health emergency terminology within national emergency legislation in responding to health emergencies. Lancet 403(10435):1504–1512

World Health Organization (2015) Framework for a Public Health Emergency Operations Centre. https://www.who.int/publications/i/item/framework-for-a-public-health-emergency-operations-centre (accessed 2 May 2024).

World Health Organization (2016) International Health Regulations (2005) – Third edition. https://www.who.int/publications/i/item/9789241580496 (accessed 22 April 2024).

World Health Organization (2024) Emergency Response Framework (ERF), Edition 2.1. https://www.who.int/publications/i/item/9789240058064 (accessed 22 April 2024).

World Health Organization (n.d.) International Health Regulations. https://www.who.int/health-topics/international-health-regulations#tab=tab_1 (accessed 25 April 2024).

Zhang X (2016) Response and management of public health emergencies. Sichuan University Press, Chengdu

Zhou Z (2020) Comparison of response systems for public health emergencies in foreign countries. People's Trib 10:48–52

Zhu F, Shen X (2017) Public health emergency: theory and practice. Southeast University Press, Nanjing

Chapter 4
Surveillance and Early Warning on Public Health Risk

4.1 Introduction to Surveillance and Early Warning for Public Health Risk

4.1.1 Introduction to Surveillance for Public Health Risk

4.1.1.1 Definition of Public Health Surveillance

As the discipline of public health continues to evolve, the concept of public health surveillance is also being refined. The academic community generally agrees that public health surveillance refers to the process of long-term, continuous, and systematic collection of public health data related to the promotion of population health, the acquirement of important public health information after analyzing and interpreting the data obtained, and the timely feedback of the information to all those who should be informed so as to guide the formulation, refinement, and evaluation of public health measures and strategies.

Early public health surveillance mainly involved the observation of the occurrence and mortality of diseases, hence the term disease surveillance. However, as the scope of surveillance expanded, it was referred to as epidemiological surveillance. Nowadays, it is generally known as public health surveillance. The earliest disease surveillance activities originated from the monitoring of infectious diseases, but with the transformation in the disease spectrum and modern medical model, the range of objects monitored has been continuously expanding, from infectious diseases primarily to many aspects including chronic diseases, injuries, occupational factors, personal behavior, and sudden public health events.

Public health surveillance has the following three basic characteristics (Zhan 2018):

A. Long-term, continuous, and systematic collection of the data on health events and health issues.

J. Liu, *Risk Management in Public Health*, Innovation in Risk Analysis,
https://doi.org/10.1007/978-981-97-6826-4_4

B. The original data must be scientifically analyzed and interpreted to obtain important public health information.
C. Health information should be promptly fed back to relevant departments and personnel for full utilization, in order to formulate, implement, evaluate, and adjust public health strategies and measures.

4.1.1.2 Scopes and Aims of Surveillance

Based on the collected public health information, public health surveillance could primarily help to understand the distribution characteristics and trends of health-related events, identify the risk factors and high-risk groups for health events, and evaluate the effectiveness of intervention strategies and measures.

Understanding the Distribution Characteristics and Trends of Health-Related Events

Through continuous and systematic public health surveillance, we can comprehensively understand the distribution characteristics and future trends of certain health-related events in specific areas or population, thereby helping to achieve the following objectives:

A. Identify the main public health issues. Policymakers expect to achieve correct and effective results when formulating public health policies and measures, so it is necessary to have an understanding of the current status of public health issues. By systematically and continuously collecting data on public health issues and analyzing the data, we can understand the occurrence, distribution characteristics, and development trends of the main diseases or health issues affecting human health, identify the current main public health issues, and carry out targeted preventive interventions.
B. Detect anomalies and identify causes, take interventions to curb the development and spread of adverse health events. Long-term and continuous regular monitoring can timely and effectively detect abnormal distribution changes of health-related events in the population, issue early warnings to relevant departments, conduct epidemiological investigations, identify the causes of changes, and take timely interventions to prevent or control further development of the events.
C. Identify high-risk groups. By comparing and analyzing the continuous and dynamic data obtained from monitoring, we can identify factors affecting the occurrence and development of diseases, and thus identifying the high-risk groups for corresponding diseases and providing a scientific basis for formulating targeted measures and effective strategies. For example, in recent years, the epidemiological characteristics of people with human immunodeficiency virus (HIV) infection or acquired immunodeficiency syndrome (AIDS) have shown an increasing proportion of young students, leading to an increasing

number of colleges and universities conducting lectures and activities to promote knowledges about HIV infection and AIDS prevention.

D. Predict the development trends of health-related events and estimate the demand for health services. By collecting and analyzing monitoring data continuously and dynamically over the long term, we can predict the future development trends and scales of health-related events based on the current prevalence, and thus estimating the future demand for health services, which could guide the production of related drugs, training of professionals, and investment in health funds.

Evaluating the Effectiveness of Interventions

Public health surveillance could obtain the long-term and continuous epidemiological characteristics of health-related events. Therefore, by comparing the changes in health-related events before and after the implementation of intervention measures at different times, we can evaluate the effectiveness of the interventions and provide a reliable basis for formulating effective public health strategies and measures.

4.1.2 Introduction to Early Warning for Public Health Risk

4.1.2.1 Definition of Early Warning

Early warning refers to the rapid identification of signals that may indicate potential acute public health events based on a surveillance information platform and using comprehensive assessment methods, and the combination of alert and response to form a complete system for controlling the spread of public health risk. Early warning is generally applied to emergencies, and its data sources include reports from health agencies, community members, and other institutions.

4.1.2.2 Scopes and Aims of Early Warning

The overall goal of early warning is to provide a foundation for rapid subsequent response by timely early detection of danger signals, in order to reduce the high incidence and mortality caused by ongoing diseases and other public health hazards (such as emerging infectious diseases, severe diseases with potential high mortality or transmission rates, diseases targeted for elimination or eradication, etc.) (Lee et al. 2018). To achieve this goal, early warning systems need to carry out continuous and rigorous monitoring.

For urgent public health emergencies, given that epidemic diseases may spread rapidly within a short time, it is a priority to establish an early warning system within the first week after the occurrence of the event. The WHO's framework for responding to emergencies recommends strengthening existing early warning systems or establishing new ones within 3 to 10 days after the occurrence of an emergency.

4.2 Surveillance and Early Warning System for Public Health Risk

4.2.1 Development of Public Health Surveillance and Early Warning System (Zhan 2018; Zhu and Shen 2017)

4.2.1.1 Development of Public Health Surveillance in Foreign Countries

The development of the discipline of epidemiology originated from the response to infectious diseases, and early public health surveillance primarily focused on infectious diseases, so the history of the development of epidemiology largely reflects the development of public health surveillance.

In 1662, the British statistician John Graunt (1620–1674) used death registration data from London churches to analyze the health status of residents, created the first life table and established the principles of birth and death statistics, which can be seen as the most primitive form of death surveillance.

In the nineteenth century, British physician and statistician William Farr (1807–1883), along with his teacher Pierre Charles Alexandre Louis, created the regular collection of population and death data, proposed many key concepts in the field of epidemiology through analysis of these data, and fed the results back to the public during his nearly 40 years as the head of the British Statistical Office.

Early public health surveillance was aimed at quarantine, mainly to detect infectious disease patients. For example, in the mid-fifteenth century, the port of Venice, Italy, required foreign ships to stay outside the port for 40 days for observation before landing; in 1741, Rhode Island, a British colony in North America, passed an ordinance that local inns were required to report travelers with acute infectious diseases such as smallpox, cholera, and yellow fever. In 1901, each state in the United States enacted relevant laws and listed the notifiable infectious diseases of the state clearly. By 1925 all states joined the national diseases reporting system. Until the 1950s, infectious diseases were always the main content of public health surveillance.

In 1943, Denmark established a cancer registration system, marking the beginning of non-communicable diseases surveillance. In 1968, at the 21st World Health Assembly, WHO clarified the position of surveillance in public health and that the scope of surveillance included all health issues, including infectious diseases. With the transformation of the disease spectrum and the medical model, the scope of monitoring has been continuously expanding, from infectious diseases to non-communicable diseases, from disease factors (e.g., behavior) to various events related to health (e.g., health service evaluation); the methods of monitoring have been continuously improved, from pure biomedical observation to using interdisciplinary methods such as sociology and behavioral science for research. This greatly enriched the information of monitoring, thus guiding public health interventions better.

After the 1990s, Internet technology developed rapidly and was applied to monitoring activities, significantly improving the efficiency of data collection and processing, and also greatly increasing the speed of information feedback, which has strongly promoted the development of public health surveillance. For example, the European Union organization realized that monitoring is an important link in the prevention and control of infectious diseases, and gradually built a network-based European Early Warning and Response System (EWRS) for communicable diseases to carry out monitoring and coordinate and unify monitoring methods throughout Europe, thereby improving the comparability and compatibility of the collected data.

4.2.1.2 Construction of Public Health Surveillance System in China

Before the founding of the People's Republic of China, there was no systematic public health surveillance system. After the establishment of China, the country established a statutory infectious disease reporting system in 1950. This is the most important and basic national infectious disease surveillance system, with the number of diseases reported increasing from 18, 25, 35, to 40 currently (including COVID-19). Since 1975, China has successively established many single-disease surveillance systems for influenza, Japanese encephalitis, meningococcal meningitis, cholera, hemorrhagic fever with renal syndrome, plague, and leptospirosis, combining national infectious disease reports with pathogen and serological monitoring in key areas and populations, significantly improving the capabilities of infectious disease surveillance and prevention in China.

In the late 1970s, Professor Guanqing He (1911—1995) proposed in 1979 to establish comprehensive disease surveillance sites in China to determine the main health issues. With the support and leadership of the former Ministry of Health, China established a long-term comprehensive surveillance system mainly for infectious diseases in 1980. In 2003, the system was transformed into the National Disease Surveillance System, adding non-communicable diseases, infant mortality rate, cause of death analysis, life expectancy and other demographic data, information on smoking and health, water and health, and the nutritional status of residents, as well as the cost-effectiveness analysis of interventions and evaluation of community health services.

Entering the 1980s, with the transformation of the disease spectrum and etiological spectrum, the scope of public health surveillance objects continued to expand, from the early focus on infectious diseases to many aspects including chronic diseases, injuries, occupational factors, behavioral risk factors, and sudden public health events. China has successively established a number of national public health surveillance systems, including the birth defect surveillance system, HIV infection sentinel surveillance system, iodine deficiency disease prevention and control surveillance system, and maternal and child health surveillance system. The outbreak of severe acute respiratory syndrome (SARS) in 2003 once again aroused the country's high attention to infectious disease epidemics and sudden public health events. China strengthened the statutory infectious disease reporting system and established a network direct reporting information platform, established a new reporting system for sudden public health events, and increased investment in public health surveillance work, improving the efficiency of the surveillance system. It has played a great role in responding to infectious diseases such as H1N1 influenza, Middle East respiratory syndrome (EMRS), and coronavirus disease 2019 (COVID-19).

4.2.2 Main Types of Public Health Surveillance and Early Warning System

As the socio-economic landscape evolves, so do the spectrum of human diseases and their causes, leading to an expansion in the types and content of public health surveillance. Currently, the types of public health surveillance mainly include disease surveillance, cause of death surveillance, hospital infection surveillance, symptom surveillance, behavioral surveillance, adverse drug reaction surveillance and so on (Zhan 2018).

4.2.2.1 Disease Surveillance

Disease surveillance is the earliest form of public health surveillance and remains one of the most fundamental and crucial components of modern disease prevention and control efforts. Disease surveillance is a type of outcome surveillance that requires clear definitions related to the diagnosis or death associated with the disease in question.

Infectious Disease Surveillance

Infectious disease surveillance is the origin of disease surveillance and is also one of its most important aspects. In 2005, the World Health Assembly reviewed and passed the International Health Regulations (IHR), which came into effect on June 15, 2007. The IHR designated five infectious diseases for international monitoring by the World Health Organization: influenza, polio, malaria, typhoid fever, and relapsing fever. Chinese infectious disease surveillance system (the statutory infectious disease reporting and feedback system) was initially established in the 1950s. With the discovery of more infectious diseases, by 2020, Chinese statutory reported infectious diseases included 2 Class A diseases, 27 Class B diseases, and 11 Class C diseases.

The purpose and content of infectious disease surveillance mainly include the following aspects:

A. Timely detection and diagnosis of cases to identify emerging infectious diseases or new public health issues and to carry out related prevention and control efforts.
B. Collection of demographic data and the distribution of infectious disease incidence and mortality cases to understand the three-dimensional distribution of infectious diseases, promptly determine the extent of disease prevalence, and implement corresponding measures to control outbreaks.
C. Monitoring the serotype, virulence, drug resistance, and other variations of pathogens, the level of population immunity, as well as the types, distribution, and pathogen-carrying status of animal hosts and vector insects, to analyze disease development trends, identify potential high-risk populations and areas, and provide a reference for the formulation of related measures and strategies.
D. Monitoring changes of the epidemics and analyzing the progress and effectiveness of public health intervention strategies or measures.

Chronic Non-Communicable Disease Surveillance

In recent years, with the changes of disease spectrum, the scope of disease surveillance in many countries has expanded to include chronic non-communicable diseases. The scope and content of surveillance vary depending on the main health issues and surveillance objectives of each country and region, and mainly include malignant tumors, cardiovascular and cerebrovascular diseases, diabetes, occupational diseases, mental disorders, birth defects, injuries, etc.

The U.S. National Cancer Institute (NCI) has been monitoring cancer since the 1970s. The U.S. CDC has been carrying out chronic disease health promotion activities since the 1980s, monitoring 10 preventable chronic diseases that severely affect the quality of life, such as coronary heart disease, diabetes, cirrhosis, alcoholism and breast cancer, etc. The first phase of the Monitoring of Trends and Determinants in Cardiovascular Disease (MONICA) program funded by WHO ran for 10 years from 1984 to 1993. The MONICA program included 27 countries, 39 centers, and 113 reporting units, covering a population of 13 million. More countries have since joined and improved the surveillance program, the main purpose of which is to monitor the occurrence and mortality of cardiovascular diseases, as well as changes in related risk factors, health services, and socio-economic development, in order to take effective action to reduce mortality due to cardiovascular diseases.

Some regions in China have carried out surveillance on chronic non-communicable diseases such as malignant tumors, cardiovascular and cerebrovascular diseases, and hypertension. For example, the Beijing Cardiopulmonary Vascular Medical Research Center (now the Beijing Institute of Cardiopulmonary and Vascular Diseases) took the lead in organizing a major collaboration in 16 provinces and cities, 19 monitoring areas in China and monitoring the development trends of cardiovascular diseases and their influencing factors. In 1984, Tianjin carried out research on the prevention and control of non-communicable "four diseases" with a focus on malignant tumors, coronary heart disease, stroke and hypertension. The "National Birth Defect Monitoring Network", established in 1986, carried out hospital-based birth defect monitoring, mainly monitoring 23 types of birth defects. In 1988, birth defect monitoring was converted into routine work by the Ministry of Health, collectively referred to as the "three-network monitoring" along with the national maternal mortality monitoring and the under-five mortality monitoring at that time. In 1996, the Ministry of Health merged these three monitoring networks (referred to as "three-network integration") and officially implemented the China Maternal and Child Health Monitoring Program. In addition, in terms of malignant tumors, the National Cancer Registration and Reporting continuously collects, preserves, organizes, analyzes, and evaluates the incidence, prevalence, mortality, diagnostic methods, tumor stage distribution, treatment methods, and survival data of malignant tumors, including population-based and hospital-based cancer registration. The former is used to evaluate the burden and development trend of tumors, provide basic data for tumor etiology and prevention research, and evaluate the effectiveness of national cancer prevention and control projects. The latter is mainly used to evaluate the effectiveness of diagnosis and treatment of cancer patients.

The contents of chronic non-communicable disease surveillance mainly include:

A. Collecting demographic data related to chronic non-communicable diseases, the situation and distribution of incidence and mortality, clarifying the three-dimensional distribution of the diseases;
B. Monitoring and surveying lifestyle and behavioral risk factors in the population, geographical, environmental, and socio-cultural (including economic) factors, as well as diet and nutrition factors to identify the influencing factors of the diseases;
C. Monitoring of genotype and genetic background factors;
D. Identification of high-risk groups;
E. Evaluation of the effectiveness of prevention and intervention measures.

Hospital Infection Surveillance

Hospital infection surveillance refers to the long-term, systematic, and continuous collection and analysis of the occurrence and distribution of hospital infections in a certain population (mainly inpatients) and their influencing factors. The results obtained are reported and fed back to relevant departments and sections to provide a scientific basis for the prevention, control, and management of hospital infections. The current "Hospital Infection Surveillance Standards" (WS/T312-2009) in China were issued by the former Ministry of Health in April 2009 and started in December of the same year. Hospital infection surveillance includes comprehensive hospital-wide surveillance targeted surveillance, as well as bacterial resistance surveillance, and antimicrobial use surveillance. The standards require that hospitals should establish an effective hospital infection surveillance and communication system, diagnose hospital infection cases promptly, analyze the risk factors for hospital infections, and take targeted prevention and control measures. It is also required that hospitals should cultivate the awareness and ability of hospital infection control professionals and clinical medical staff to identify hospital infection outbreaks. When an outbreak occurs, they should analyze the source and route of infection, take effective measures, and report to the health administrative department within the specified time according to different situations of hospital infection outbreaks.

Cause of Death Surveillance

The purpose of cause of death surveillance is to understand the mortality rate and cause of death distribution in the population. Through the statistical analysis, it can reflect the health status of the monitored population and determine the main causes of death and the focus of disease prevention and control in different periods.

Cause of death surveillance is a fundamental task of continuously and systematically collecting death data of the population and conducting comprehensive analysis to study the level of death, causes of death and trends. In 1989 and 1992, China established the National Maternal Mortality Surveillance Network and the National Under-Five Mortality Surveillance Network, respectively. The monitoring information is used to reflect the health status of women and children in China. The Chinese CDC formulated and issued the "National Disease Surveillance System Cause of Death Monitoring Work Standards (Trial)" and the "National Cause of Death Registration Information Network Reporting Work Standards (Trial)" in 2007, making the cause of death Surveillance work more standardized. Among them, the Death Medical Certificate is an important voucher for cause of death reporting and statistical analysis, and correct cause of death determination is the most important basis for cause of death surveillance.

4.2.2.2 Syndromic Surveillance

Syndromic surveillance, also known as syndrome surveillance, is a monitoring method that provides early detection, early warning and rapid response to the occurrence or prevalence of a particular type of disease through the long-term, continuous and systematic collection of the frequency of specific clinical syndromes or disease-related phenomena. Syndromic surveillance can actively monitor the initial stages of public health events, especially suitable for emerging diseases, of which the etiology is unclear and there are no definitive diagnostic methods available in clinical practice. It provides a scientific basis for relevant personnel to take timely and effective prevention and control measures.

The Chinese syndromic surveillance systems mainly include:

Influenza-Like Illness (ILI) Surveillance System

In June 2005, China started influenza-like illness surveillance with the aim of establishing a standardized, sensitive, efficient, and nationwide influenza surveillance network to grasp the dynamics of the influenza epidemic timely, identify current influenza strains and new variant strains, and provide information for health departments and related units to make early warning and predictions and formulate effective measures. The ultimate goal is to prevent influenza pandemics, reduce excess mortality, and contribute to the recommendation and production of global influenza vaccines. The subjects of ILI surveillance system are influenza-like cases visiting medical institutions in monitoring sites. Specimens were collected from influenza-like cases within 3 days of the onset of illness. Influenza-like cases were defined as acute respiratory infections with temperature > 38 °C, accompanied by coughing, or symptoms such as sore throat and generalized pain. The monitoring period is stipulated as six months per year for northern provinces (from October 1 to March 31 of the following year), while full-year monitoring in the southern provinces. During 2009–2010, the ILI surveillance system played a key role in detecting, confirming, and preventing the pandemic of H1N1 influenza in China.

Unexplained Pneumonia Surveillance System

After the SARS outbreak in 2003, China began to establish a surveillance system for unexplained pneumonia. The purpose of the national surveillance of unexplained pneumonia cases is to identify potential SARS cases, avian influenza cases in humans, and other infectious respiratory diseases, issue early warnings to relevant units and populations, and take appropriate prevention and control measures to prevent the spread of the epidemic and the potential avian influenza outbreak.

Rash and Fever Illness Surveillance System

Measles monitoring is a type of the Rash and Fever Illness Surveillance System. Strengthening measles monitoring is one of the main strategies for measles elimination. To cooperate with the implementation of the "2006–2012 National Plan for the Elimination of Measles" and strengthening measles monitoring work, the measles surveillance plan was revised in February 2009. Since then, the targets of measles monitoring are defined as individuals with fever, rash, and at least one of the following symptoms: cough, catarrhal rhinitis, or conjunctivitis; or patients suspected of measles by the responsible reporters for infectious diseases.

Infectious Diarrhea Surveillance System

Infectious diarrhea is a group of intestinal infectious diseases mainly characterized by diarrhea, caused by various pathogens such as bacteria, viruses, and parasites. The intestinal clinics in all medical institutions are the main surveillance sites for infectious diarrhea in China, and they have gradually expanded to include departments such as pediatric infectious diseases and emergency departments in recent years. The surveillance cases (diarrhea-like cases) of the Infectious Diarrhea Surveillance System are defined as children aged ≥ 1 year and adults who have bowel movements ≥ 3 times/day, accompanied by a change in stool character, presenting as loose stools, watery stools, mucoid stools, or bloody mucoid stools.

From the contents of the above syndromic surveillance systems, it can be seen that the symptoms focused on by the syndromic surveillance system do not depend on diagnostic results but on non-specific symptoms. The purpose is to detect suspicious diseases as early as possible and take corresponding measures. As different diseases may have similar symptoms, non-specific symptom surveillance may lead to an overestimation of the epidemic, causing unnecessary panic and economic losses. However, since the appearance of various symptoms always precedes the diagnosis of the disease, the sensitivity of disease detection can be improved through syndromic surveillance. Especially in dealing with sudden public health events such as foodborne diseases and bioterrorism, syndromic surveillance has played an important role and therefore has attracted more and more attention.

4.2.2.3 Behavior and Behavior Risk Factors Surveillance

Behavior and behavior risk factors surveillance focuses on the causes of public health events. Studies have shown that unhealthy personal behaviors and lifestyles are closely related to the occurrence and development of chronic diseases, accidental injuries and sexually transmitted diseases such as AIDS. For example, smoking, diets high in fat and salt and low in protein, lack of physical activity and lack of protective measures (such as not wearing seat belts) are risk factors for chronic diseases and traffic accidents, all of which are referred to as behavior risk factors.

With the transformation of disease spectrum of humanity, promoting changes in human behavior has become a major strategy for the prevention and control of chronic diseases, injuries, and sexually transmitted diseases. An increasing number of countries around the world have also realized the importance of behavior risk factors surveillance. The United States, the United Kingdom, Canada, Germany, Italy, and other countries have established national Behavior Risk Factors Surveillance System (BRFSS) to collect behavior data related to chronic diseases, injuries, and preventable infectious diseases, such as smoking, alcohol abuse, poor dietary habits and insufficient physical activity regularly. Chinese BRFSS is one of the disease surveillance systems hosted by the Chinese Academy of Preventive Medicine, established in 1996 as part of the Chinese World Bank's seventh health loan project—the health promotion sub-project. The entire surveillance system covers cities such as

Shanghai, Beijing, Tianjin, Chengdu, Luoyang, Liuzhou, Weihai, and Kunming in Yunnan Province, and is a household survey monitoring system based on cities. The purpose is to collect behavior risk factors data related to the occurrence, development, or death of diseases in the populations aged 16 to 69 through continuous monthly household surveys, and provide a strong reference for government departments to formulate and evaluate prevention strategies and interventions.

Currently, the surveys of Chinese behavior risk factor surveillance system include a core questionnaire and additional questionnaires. The former focuses on the main risk factors for chronic diseases, including information on smoking, alcohol abuse, lack of physical activity, unhealthy diet, and unsafe sexual behavior. The main objective is to understand people's knowledge, attitudes, and behaviors related to these risk factors. Each city is required to conduct surveys in the core questionnaire, with Yunnan Province only surveying the demographic characteristics, health services, and STD/AIDS sections. Additional questionnaires are designed by each city to add questions or other elements to these 12 sections according to the situation of the city, based on the core questionnaire.

4.2.2.4 Surveillance for Other Public Health Events

Due to the rich content of public health events, there are many types of surveillance systems established for them, including, in addition to the Disease Surveillance, Syndromic Surveillance, and Behavior and Behavior Risk Factors Surveillance mentioned above, drug adverse reaction surveillance, nutrition and food safety surveillance, sudden public health events surveillance, environmental surveillance, etc.

4.3 Surveillance and Early Warning Methods for Public Health Risk

4.3.1 Types of Methods for Public Health Surveillance (M'ikanatha et al. 2013)

4.3.1.1 Passive Surveillance

Passive surveillance is a system where subordinate units routinely report surveillance data to higher authorities, who then passively receive the information. This type of surveillance is primarily implemented in accordance with relevant laws and regulations. In China, systems such as the infectious disease reporting information system, the public health emergency reporting system, and the spontaneous reporting system for adverse drug reactions are all examples of passive surveillance.

4.3.1.2 Active Surveillance

Active surveillance refers to surveys specifically conducted by higher-level agencies to collect information due to the special needs of public health events such as disease prevention and control. In China, monitoring of vaccination rates, investigations into underreporting of infectious diseases to correct surveillance data, and monitoring activities for certain key or emerging diseases or behavior factors are all considered active surveillance.

4.3.1.3 Routine Report

It involves regular monitoring and reporting on diseases or various health-related issues as stipulated by health administrative departments. For example, Chinese infectious disease reporting information system involves reporting on infectious diseases as mandated by laws and regulations.

4.3.1.4 Sentinel Surveillance

Sentinel surveillance is conducted to gain a clearer understanding of the distribution of certain diseases across different regions and populations as well as their influencing factors. Based on the epidemiological characteristics of the diseases being monitored, a certain number of representative areas and (or) populations are selected to carry out continuous monitoring on according to a unified surveillance plan. For instance, HIV sentinel surveillance involves selecting representative areas and high-risk groups for HIV, conducting continuous, fixed-site, timed, and quantified HIV antibody testing according to a unified monitoring plan, and simultaneously collecting information on high-risk behaviors related to the spread of AIDS among the monitored populations. This allows for the acquisition of data on the HIV infection status, behavior risk factors and trends in different areas and among different populations.

4.3.2 Process of Surveillance and Early Warning for Public Health Risk

The main processes of public health surveillance include four key components: data collection, data management and analysis, information feedback and information utilization.

4.3.2.1 Data Collection

Data should be collected systematically and comprehensively according to the specific objectives of the surveillance system, thus ensuring the completeness, representativeness, and accuracy of the obtained data. Before starting data collection, unified standards, methods, and standardized procedures should be established. The main contents of the surveillance data include:

A. Demographic data;
B. Disease incidence or mortality data in the population;
C. Laboratory test data, such as etiological and serological information;
D. Risk factor information, such as smoking, occupational exposure, etc.;
E. Records of intervention measures, such as vaccine distribution, iodized salt, etc.;
F. Special investigation reports;
G. Other relevant information, such as environmental and climatic data.

4.3.2.2 Data Management and Analysis

Data management refers to the process of carefully checking and organizing the collected surveillance data, understanding the sources and collection methods, and discarding erroneous or irreparably incomplete data to ensure the completeness and accuracy of the data once again.

Data analysis means using appropriate statistical methods to transform data into relevant indicators and interpreting them. By this way, the distribution characteristics, patterns, trends, and influencing factors of the public health events being monitored can be obtained.

4.3.2.3 Information Feedback

The information obtained from monitoring data collection, analysis, and interpretation must be fully fed back to be effective. In a complete surveillance system, it is necessary to establish channels for information feedback, building a bridge between public health issues and public health interventions, so that all units and individuals who should understand the monitoring information can obtain it in a timely manner to respond quickly to the epidemic, clarify work priorities, and research directions. Information feedback can be vertical and horizontal, with vertical feedback including reporting to health administrative departments and reporting to lower-level monitoring institutions. Horizontal feedback includes feedback to relevant medical and health institutions, research units, communities, and residents.

Information feedback can be regularly distributed in the form of bulletins, or it can be provided through telephone, Internet, and other forms. For example, WHO regularly organizes and analyzes various monitoring data and compiles them into the Weekly Epidemiological Record. There are daily, weekly, monthly, and annual reports on related disease surveillance in China, such as infectious disease surveillance reports and maternal and child health reports.

4.3.2.4 Information Utilization

The value of collected information is only realized when it is fully utilized. The ultimate goal of establishing a surveillance system is to formulate public health strategies and measures through the collection, processing, and utilization of information to prevent and control the occurrence and development of public health events. The information obtained from surveillance can be used to understand the distribution characteristics of health events, predict trends, identify major health issues, and evaluate the effectiveness of interventions, providing a basis for formulating strategies and measures to prevent and control diseases.

4.3.3 Techniques of Surveillance and Early Warning for Public Health Events

In the monitoring process, the correct use of monitoring methods and technologies helps to improve the quality and efficiency of monitoring. With the development of modern information technology, public health surveillance increasingly applies technologies such as computer networks and geographic information systems, which facilitate the collection, management, analysis, transmission, and feedback of monitoring information, thereby greatly improving the work efficiency of the surveillance system and making the formulation of public health strategies and the implementation of intervention measures timelier.

4.3.3.1 Case Registry

It refers to the discovery, detection, diagnosis, and registration of cases related to monitoring in daily work. It is the foundation of monitoring work and an essential part of disease and cause-of-death surveillance.

4.3.3.2 Unrelated Surveillance

It is used when the purpose of surveillance is merely to understand the prevalence of a disease in the population, rather than to identify specific cases. In this case, data collected by other studies can be utilized without identifying individuals for surveillance. For example, collecting blood samples from hospital laboratories or health check-ups for a certain population and conducting HIV testing without identifying personal identities. This type of surveillance can avoid ethical issues to a certain extent.

4.3.3.3 Record Linkages

Connecting data from two different sources to form a new database for statistical analysis, thereby obtaining more valuable monitoring information, which is called record linkages. For instance, birth records may contain information about future morbidity or mortality, while infant death records may lack birth weight data. However, linking these two sets of data can provide mortality rate information for infants of different birth weights.

4.3.3.4 Online Collection of Surveillance Information

By utilizing telephone and computer-assisted network surveys, investigators can obtain higher-quality survey data in a shorter time and at a lower cost. The obtained data can be used directly by various statistical software for automated data management and automated statistical analysis, thus completing the collection and analysis of monitoring information in a quick and easy manner. Network surveys, also known as online surveys, refer to the online and intelligent transformation of traditional paper-based surveys and analysis methods through the Internet and its survey systems, which can greatly expand the number of survey participants and geographical scope, save survey costs, and improve the efficiency of data management and statistical analysis.

4.3.3.5 Internet Direct Reporting System

With the rapid development and popularization of computer network technology, public health surveillance is increasingly being carried out through the establishment and adoption of Internet direct reporting systems. In Chinese public health emergency surveillance system and the statutory infectious disease reporting information system, Internet direct reporting system has been basically achieved at the county and township levels, which has greatly shortened the time for information transmission and laid the foundation for rapid data processing.

4.3.3.6 Automatic Early Warning Technology

Early warning refers to the issuance of an alarm based on abnormal information found in monitoring, such as an unusual increase in cases of a certain disease, so that relevant departments and populations that may be affected by the event can respond in a timely manner. Automatic early warning technology uses mathematical models and Internet technology to determine warning thresholds through specific algorithms, automatically detect and discover possible abnormal information (above the threshold), and issue an early warning signal. It is important to note that the level of the warning threshold directly affects the sensitivity and specificity of the early warning signal, so further analysis and verification are needed for the suspicious events indicated by the early warning signal.

4.3.3.7 Geographic Information System (GIS)

GIS is a computer system for collecting, storing, managing, analyzing, describing, and applying data and information related to the spatial geographic distribution of the entire or part of the Earth's surface (including the atmosphere). The use of GIS can make public health surveillance data more visually represented in regional distribution, which helps to analyze the impact of geographical environment and climate factors on public health issues. Currently, GIS has been widely used in disease surveillance and prevention such as vector-borne disease monitoring, etiology and risk factor analysis, environmental health research, health service utilization, and public health emergency events.

4.4 Surveillance and Early Warning Information Release and Public Communication

4.4.1 Definition of Surveillance and Early Warning Information Release

The results derived from the analysis of public health surveillance data should be published in an open form. This not only allows decision-makers to understand the surveillance reports and use them for decision-making but also raises public awareness of public health emergencies, enabling a faster and better response. Surveillance and early warning information release refers to issuing timely and accurate warning reports to the public based on scientific monitoring and prediction of public health events. This raises people's vigilance about public health emergencies, prepares them to deal with such events, and reduces the harm caused by the events.

4.4.2 Methods of Surveillance and Early Warning Information Release

Considering the different information requirements and usage methods of the audience, surveillance and early warning information release can adopt various approaches. Under normal circumstances, public access to databases must comply with privacy permissions, and access conditions and publishers should be set in advance. Data can be obtained through various electronic media forms, ranging from structured surveillance data suitable for general analysis to original data files that allow more detailed and professional analysis. The advantages of the Internet, chart software, and geographic distribution software have facilitated the acquisition and understanding of existing information. The main target audience for surveillance information includes public health professionals and healthcare providers. An increasing number of healthcare purchasers and consumers are also paying attention to surveillance data to understand the quality of medical services, thereby using surveillance information to strengthen the management of the healthcare system. The information provided should be analyzed and interpreted, and some usage recommendations should be offered. Charts and geographic distribution analysis methods should be widely used to facilitate efficient reading of reports and better understanding. Social media plays an important role in secondary dissemination, promoting the spread of surveillance information and health surveillance results. The media play an important role in promoting and strengthening the dissemination of health information, innovate technologies should be applied, such as the extensive application of audio-visual technology.

4.4.3 Standards and Contents of Surveillance and Early Warning Information Release

4.4.3.1 Standards of Surveillance and Early Warning Information Release

Information dissemination should be carried out in accordance with the principles of being timely and proactive, accurately grasping the situation, emphasizing effects and eliminating concealment of information. Proactively and promptly track the progress of emergencies, assess the development of the situation, and strive to release information on infectious disease outbreaks and public health emergencies at the earliest opportunity to effectively guide public opinion and prevent or reduce speculative and distorted reporting.

Use simple and understandable language to disseminate core information that includes facts, attitudes, and measures that the public should adopt to meet the needs of the media and the public for information and prevent or quell social panic.

Avoid situations where information is released by multiple authorities or where messages conflict. If such situations arise, take swift measures to facilitate rapid and effective handling of the emergency.

Adopt different communication strategies according to the different stages of the emergency and the different groups of people. While announcing information on public health emergencies, it is necessary to publicize the preventive and control measures taken by the party, government, and various departments, as well as relevant scientific knowledge.

4.4.3.2 Contents of Surveillance and Early Warning Information Release

Notifiable Infectious Disease Epidemics

The contents of notifiable infectious disease epidemics include the overall situation of Class A and B infectious diseases, the distribution of major infectious diseases, the control of major epidemics, and the basic situation of Class C infectious diseases.

Case Information of Public Health Emergencies

Information on public health emergencies released in individual case form. It mainly includes: the nature and cause of the public health emergency; the location and scope of the public health emergency; the incidence, casualties, and the scope of personnel involved in the public health emergency; measures and control of the public health emergency; and the lifting of compulsory measures in the area where the public health emergency occurred.

Overall Information of Public Health Emergencies

Information on public health emergencies released in an overall form, mainly including: the overall and distribution situation of acute major infectious diseases, acute food poisoning, acute occupational poisoning, cluster diseases of unknown causes and other public health emergencies that severely affect public health, including the number of occurrences, the number of people affected, and the emergency response situation of various levels of public health emergencies.

4.5 Opportunities and Challenges for Public Health Surveillance Systems

4.5.1 Opportunities for Public Health Surveillance Systems

4.5.1.1 International Cooperation

In the context of globalization, cross-border public health cooperation has become possible. Through international cooperation, it is possible to achieve information sharing, resource coordination, and technical support. Information sharing refers to the sharing of key information across borders and institutions to gain a more comprehensive understanding of global health threats. In terms of resource coordination, international partners can provide funding and resources for the development and maintenance of public health surveillance systems. Additionally, international organizations and developed countries can provide technical support to help countries with limited resources establish and strengthen their public health surveillance systems.

4.5.1.2 Technological Advancements

Advancements in technology have made the development of electronic early warning, alert, and response (EWAR) tools possible (World Health Organization 2022). Currently available fully electronic EWAR tools include EWARS-in-a-box, electronic Disease Early Warning System (eDEWS), and District Health Information Software version 2 (DHIS2) and so on. These tools support every aspect from data collection to dissemination, including but not limited to: data collection, data management, alert generation and management, data analysis and visualization, Geographic Information Systems (GIS), and mobile data collection. These tools have been applied in various countries and institutions, supporting the surveillance and response efforts for diseases such as Ebola, COVID-19, measles, dengue fever, and diphtheria. Efforts can continue to be made to develop and improve electronic EWAR tools globally, in order to enhance the efficiency of data collection, management, and analysis, thereby accelerating the response to public health threats.

4.5.2 Challenges for Public Health Surveillance Systems

4.5.2.1 Surveillance Systems Need to Be Optimized

Infectious disease surveillance systems started earlier and a relatively complete network direct reporting system has been established. However, the construction of chronic non-communicable disease surveillance systems still needs to be advanced.

With urbanization, aging of the population and changes in people's lifestyles, chronic non-communicable diseases have become the main public health problems endangering human health. But the national unified surveillance systems for chronic non-communicable diseases are still under construction, and the existing surveillance systems are not fully capable of dealing with the challenges that chronic non-communicable diseases bring to public health. For example, there are a lot of data from national-level chronic diseases and risk factor surveys or provincial-level monitoring, and there might be overlaps in the content of the surveillance systems and related surveys, but a sharing mechanism for multi-source data has not yet been formed. In addition, in recent years, frequent food safety accidents, drug safety accidents, occupational safety accidents, and major epidemics in various countries have seriously endangered the health and life safety of the people and hindered the stable and healthy development of the social economy. The construction process of surveillance systems for major epidemics, food safety, drug safety, and occupational safety needs to be accelerated.

4.5.2.2 Surveillance Capability Needs to Be Improved

At present, some public health surveillance systems are not yet perfect and there are still situations of delayed reporting, false reporting, underreporting and misreporting. This might be due to:

A. Medical institutions, as the outpost units for discovering, reporting, and treating patients, lack of training for staff, leading to personnel responsible for filling in and reporting not being able to use the system skillfully and accurately, and not paying enough attention to reporting.
B. Staff in some medical institutions are not well aware of the risks of emerging infectious diseases, are not sensitive enough, and have a mentality of misjudging or concealing. Compared with hospitals specializing in infectious diseases, some general hospitals lack reserves of personnel related to the prevention, control, and treatment of infectious diseases. In emergencies, it is difficult for clinicians to carry out infectious disease prevention and control work in a planned manner, in addition to dealing with routine medical treatment.
C. The level of informatization of different regions and medical institutions at different levels is uneven. Some monitoring sites still use oral, email and paper reporting cards to register information, and then hand it over to special personnel for electronic reporting, which takes a long time and is labor-intensive.
D. The coordination and cooperation between departments need to be strengthened. Chinese infectious diseases surveillance system follows a "vertical centralized" information reporting regime, that is, the first person to know the infectious disease reports it level by level and is subject to territorial restrictions. Some medical institutions responsible for reporting information are not affiliated with the disease control departments responsible for reviewing the reported information, or the linkage between departments is not strong, leading to a lack

of cooperation between the departments and affecting the timeliness of the report. An effective coordination mechanism should be established between different institutions and departments to ensure the smooth operation of the surveillance and early warning systems. This involves ensuring that all personnel follow standardized processes and there is a clear channel for data reporting and feedback.

4.5.2.3 Surveillance Technology Needs to Be Developed

The continuous emergence of emerging infectious diseases and public health emergencies has put forward higher requirements for the data sources, monitoring methods, early warning capabilities, and rapid response processes of the surveillance systems. There is an urgent need to promote the construction of multi-source big data management systems and the research and development and application of multi-point triggered monitoring and early warning technologies. In the early stage of the construction of Chinese infectious disease surveillance system, paper infectious disease reporting cards were used for reporting at all levels, which was time-consuming and labor-intensive. Entering the twenty-first century, with the advancement of technology, the infectious disease surveillance system has gradually changed to a network direct reporting system, greatly accelerating the response process of relevant departments. However, the existing network direct reporting system still has shortcomings. In the information age, facing big data from multiple sources, the surveillance system still needs further optimization. For example, in medical institutions, it is necessary to establish a system that can collect, process, analyze, and interpret a large amount of data from multiple sources, and comprehensively use information from hospital information management systems, laboratory report management systems, medical image management systems, and electronic medical record systems, etc., to establish an infectious disease reporting management system through intelligent information sharing, that is, automatically filling out the infectious disease reporting cards through clinical doctor diagnosis, laboratory and imaging test results, which helps to avoid delayed reporting, underreporting and other phenomena.

4.5.2.4 Public Health Surveillance Systems Need Increased Resource Investment

In the future, public health will face huge challenges. We are now facing serious threats, such as weather disasters and widespread influenza outbreaks, as well as man-made disasters and wars, which can quickly increase the incidence and mortality of diseases in the population in time and space. At the same time, we are facing such an urgent reality that brings a large number of diseases and deaths in a more dramatic way. For example, the prevalence of obesity, the high burden of smoking-related diseases, public health problems brought by extreme poverty, and the resurgence and emergence of AIDS and other neglected infectious diseases. Therefore, sufficient financial, human, and operational resource investment are needed to support the implementation of the public health risk surveillance system. They include allocating sufficient budget for the entire surveillance and early warning system to ensure the sustainability of the system, ensuring that there are enough multidisciplinary professionals to coordinate, and providing necessary operational resources for professionals, such as safety, transportation, communication device, data collection and management tools, and medical and laboratory equipment. These elements are crucial to ensure that the public health risk surveillance system can provide early warning and timely response in emergencies.

In terms of human resources, personnel in public health surveillance and early warning system must be versatile and agile, and have the ability to deal with various aspects of community health problems. It is necessary to provide structured training and supportive supervision for all personnel involved in public health risk surveillance to ensure that all professionals, including health facility staff, community volunteers, and data management personnel, understand how to perform their roles and responsibilities. Continuous supportive supervision helps staff improve work performance, encourages open two-way communication, and establishes team approaches to promote problem-solving. Training, employing, and maintaining public health surveillance professionals require systematic approaches, but relevant information is still missing. At the same time, in resource-constrained situations, training and supervision may need to rely on remote methods, which may require the use of mobile technology to achieve remote training and supervision.

References

Lee LM, Teutsch SM, Thacker SB, St. Louis ME (2018) Principles and practice of public health surveillance, Third Edition. USA: Oxford University Press

M'ikanatha NM, Lynfield R, Van Beneden CA, et al. (2013) Infectious disease surveillance. USA: Wiley-Blackwell

World Health Organization (2022) Early warning alert and response in emergencies: an operational guide. Geneva: World Health Organization. https://www.who.int/publications/i/item/9789240063587 (accessed 9 May 2024)

Zhan S (2018) Epidemiology. People's Medical Publishing House, China Beijing, pp 177–189

Zhu F, Shen X (2017) Public health emergency response: theory and practice. Southeast University Press, China Jiangsu

Chapter 5
Public Health Risk Management and Decision-Making

5.1 Introduction to Public Health Risk Management and Decision-Making

Risk management is a highly systematic, professional, scientific, and comprehensive task. It is an important foundation for achieving "prevention-oriented and moving control measures upstream" in infectious disease prevention and control. It is also a scientific management method that helps enhance the predictability, specificity, and scientific nature of infectious disease prevention and control. Starting with the "risk" before the outbreak of major infectious diseases, scientifically analyze the formation and evolution mechanism of major infectious disease outbreaks, conduct dynamic monitoring, risk assessment, and early warning management of potential major infectious disease risks, and promote the management of major infectious diseases from a "post-event disposal" to a "full-cycle management" paradigm shift.

According to the life cycle of risk, risk management can be divided into: planning preparation, risk identification, risk analysis, risk evaluation, and risk disposal. These stages are cyclic, forming a complete, continuous, and dynamic risk management process (see Chapter 1, Sect. 5).

5.2 Theories and Approaches of Public Health Emergency Decision-Making

In many types of emergencies, public health emergencies receive widespread attention due to their broad impact, and the depth and duration of their impact often exceed other types of emergencies. Its characteristics are uncertainty, complexity, and unpredictability. To reduce casualties and economic losses caused by public health emergencies, decision-makers need to choose the best emergency plan from a series of alternatives. This process is called emergency decision-making (EDM).

J. Liu, *Risk Management in Public Health*, Innovation in Risk Analysis,
https://doi.org/10.1007/978-981-97-6826-4_5

In EDM, generating appropriate alternatives and choosing the best emergency plan will help reduce the adverse effects of emergencies.

Before implementing EWAR (Early Warning Alert and Response), a rapid assessment must be conducted with the aim of proposing a set of actionable recommendations to establish a system suitable for specific emergencies and contexts. As needed, the rapid assessment is led by the national public health authorities (or designated relevant departments) with the support of the World Health Organization and other partners.

Rapid assessment involves a series of key steps to determine the status of priority diseases, the geographical scope of surveillance, existing surveillance capabilities, and current logistical and resource needs.

5.2.1 Determine the Geographic Area and Population Covered by Surveillance

Assess which populations are affected, whether there are any vulnerable groups or hidden populations, where the population has migrated to, and when and where further population movements may occur. Drawing a map will help determine the boundaries of the surveillance geographic area.

5.2.2 Determine the Timeline and Geographic Scope of the Rapid Assessment

Develop a high-level assessment plan that outlines the timeline for the main activities to be completed, as well as the overall geographic scope of the areas/populations to be included in the rapid assessment. The time for conducting a rapid assessment should not exceed three days, including design and recommendation formulation. To cover a larger geographic area, the rapid assessment team can be expanded to include contact points of the EWAR system, covering all affected areas or provinces. Some areas may be difficult to access due to insecurity and/or infrastructure damage caused by natural disasters. The feasibility of actual access to the site should be balanced. If possible, consider contacting the contact points by phone, radio, or internet to avoid missing any aspects in the assessment. Alternatively, sampling a representative set of areas and generalizing the results may be sufficient.

5.2.3 Review Key Information Sources and Establish Community Consultation Mechanisms

Where possible, collect key documents on the proposed surveillance area that may be provided by national public health authorities (or equivalent bodies), the World Health Organization, non-governmental organizations, or health and water project groups. These reports help analyze current health threats and the capabilities of the current surveillance system. The epidemiological profile of infectious diseases in the area, including prevalent diseases and environmental hazards. The profile will need to be updated to consider the current emergency, including risk factors (such as living conditions and disease prevalence of displaced persons). Document existing surveillance systems to understand how they actually operate and their overall effectiveness. This may include weekly epidemiological reports, outbreak investigation reports, surveillance tools (such as local case definitions, case and laboratory report forms, standard operating procedures, digital tools), and previous surveillance assessments. Document health system and health manpower capabilities before the emergency (such as routine vaccination coverage, existing health manpower).

Document the impact and extent of the ongoing emergency, including information on the impact of the crisis, affected residents and displaced populations (and their scale), and geographic scope. These reports may include rapid health assessments, public health assessments, health resource availability monitoring system reports, integrated outbreak analysis reports, vaccination coverage estimates, and population estimate reports.

Provide a list of potential partners providing primary care, including non-governmental organizations, civil society organizations, private sector organizations, and government units. Secondary disruptions to national health care services and increased demand for services may require support from multiple partners to fill gaps in health care and gaps in EWAR's detection and reporting of acute public health events. A list of partners, health and water project team members, and a health team 3/4W matrix (who is doing what, where, and when) will be helpful. Informal interviews with key staff at all levels responsible for planning surveillance systems or interacting with surveillance systems will help identify key strengths and gaps. This may include staff managing national and provincial/state level surveillance systems, as well as health and other frontline workers supporting event/case detection in health care institutions and affected communities. Discussions should focus on key areas (i.e., priority diseases and conditions, current geographic scope of surveillance, unresolved logistical and resource needs), including informal practices and mechanisms.

5.2.4 *Determine Priority Epidemic Diseases, Conditions, and Hazards*

Before establishing EWAR, a risk assessment of potential acute public health events should be conducted to identify epidemic diseases, conditions, and environmental hazards that can lead to outbreaks or acute public health emergencies. Alternatively, they may lead to a significant increase in morbidity and/or mortality in communities affected by emergencies. The generated disease set should include a maximum of 8–12 key diseases and conditions that match potential risks in the emergency-affected population and are included in EWAR monitoring. These diseases and conditions will be primarily recorded as syndromes (i.e., a set of signs and symptoms). In certain environments, probable/confirmed cases (such as malaria rapid diagnostic test positive cases) may be included. Table 5.1 lists examples of diseases and conditions that can be prioritized for different emergencies. Note that risks may change over time, so additional syndromes (such as Zika below) may be added when these risks become apparent. Conversely, when EWAR is intended to strengthen monitoring of a specific outbreak, only one disease may be monitored (such as the Ebola virus disease outbreak monitoring in the Democratic Republic of Congo). Remember, not all infectious diseases have epidemic potential or are suitable for monitoring by EWAR. Infectious diseases such as HIV/AIDS and tuberculosis are usually not the focus of EWAR and are captured through specialized clinical surveillance and related surveillance systems. The process of determining syndrome priorities includes three steps. Narrow down the scope based on event type and related disease risk. Assess the vulnerability of the population (based on pathogen, host, and environmental factors). Describe the likelihood and potential impact of each potential disease.

5.2.5 *Propose Targeted Implementation Recommendations*

I. A concise and focused analysis of key issues related to EWAR capabilities should be conducted to identify overall gaps that require external support. The results should be integrated in the following ways to maximize communication with key stakeholders and humanitarian partners.

- A brief written report (2–3 pages) to document key findings, including: the population to be covered and the geographic scope of surveillance, key diseases and conditions to be monitored, and existing capabilities and gaps that need to be urgently addressed before implementation.
- Face-to-face briefing on the survey results to EWAR partners (i.e., different departments of the national public health authorities (or equivalent bodies), Ministry of Health, health, water project, and other groups, and donors).

Table 5.1 Examples of priority diseases and syndromes in different emergencies

Large-scale displacement in Cox's Bazaar, Bangladesh, 2017	Cyclone Winston, Fiji, 2016	Humanitarian crises in the Eastern Mediterranean Region
12 syndromes: • Acute watery diarrhoea (AWD) • Acute bloody diarrhoea • Acute jaundice syndrome • Suspected meningitis • Measles/rubella • Acute flaccid paralysis (AFP) • Acute respiratory infection • Suspected haemorrhagic fever • Malaria • Unexplained fever • Neonatal tetanus • Adult tetanus	9 syndromes: • AWD • Acute bloody diarrhoea • Acute jaundice syndrome • Suspected meningitis • Acute fever and rash • Prolonged fever • Influenza-like illness • Suspected dengue • Zika-like illness (added 3 weeks after surveillance started)	8 syndromes (on average) • Cholera • Dysentery • Hepatitis • Meningitis • Measles • Pneumonia • Polio • Haemorrhagic fever

II. The survey results should clearly indicate the current level of ability to detect and respond to outbreaks, identify specific gaps hindering EWAR, and make recommendations on how to bridge these gaps. The main recommendations should clearly specify the following main objectives.

- Utilize existing surveillance systems to fully identify gaps in meeting EWAR core functions, namely: human resources (such as core staff, training, and supervision); supplies (communication, computers, tablets) and supplementary products (laboratory); and transportation requirements (considering training and supervision for specimen transportation and support).
- Recommend urgently needed resources and deployment for new EWAR systems and coordination mechanisms. In this case, without a minimum reporting network, health institutions must be briefly introduced on how to conduct surveillance.

5.3 Domains of Interest on Public Health Emergency Decision-Making

The purpose of the risk assessment for public health emergencies is as follows: to understand the early detection capabilities for public health events. Identify parts of the core functions that need to be strengthened. Through the above two points, assess whether a new EWAR system is needed, or what inputs are needed.

The EWAR preparedness assessment (where available) will help quickly identify and verify existing capabilities of the surveillance system to support EWAR functions, thereby serving decision-making. The following areas should be rapidly assessed, with a focus on identifying basic gaps in core functions where action can be taken. The most important function from the start is outbreak detection capability. Documents and informal interviews can be analyzed to answer the following questions.

5.3.1 Surveillance People

A. Who are the affected populations (for example, internally displaced persons, refugees, and other residents affected by the crisis)? Where are they located? If in refugee camps and informal settlements, how long will they be open? Are there plans for population migration in the near future?
B. Are there up-to-date population estimates for these communities? Have they been mapped to specific geographical areas?
C. Are there severe insecurity situations that hinder humanitarian aid and their access to medical services?
D. Can the district/provincial health system reach these populations, and does it provide sufficient health coverage?
E. Are there non-governmental organizations, emergency medical teams, private healthcare facilities, and/or traditional healers supporting these populations' healthcare services? Do they have a way to participate in district/provincial surveillance?

5.3.2 Diseases and Conditions Under Surveillance

A. Does the district/provincial surveillance system already include priority diseases and conditions generated by epidemiological risk assessments in emergencies?
B. Does the existing surveillance system have the ability to detect emerging diseases? For example, is there an EBS? Is laboratory surveillance and communication in place?
C. Have health and other frontline workers been trained to detect key diseases and report according to standardized SOPs?
D. Is there a network between local, national, and regional reference laboratories to provide rapid collection, transportation, and testing of laboratory samples? Which diseases qualify for rapid detection or confirmation through district/provincial laboratories?

5.3.3 Early Warning and Surveillance

A. Does the surveillance system include weekly or more frequent reporting of routine surveillance, i.e., IBS, as a source of early warning data, according to SOPs and actual conditions?

B. Is there a list of diseases with appropriate case definitions under EWAR?
C. Does it include any form of EBS as a source of early warning data (e.g., community health workers reporting suspected events, community hotlines, rural community leaders, humanitarian partners, immediate reporting by health facilities)? Who is the focus of each source?
D. What data collection tools are used for unstructured event data from case data or listed health facility data sample data (e.g., registering rumors, telephone hotlines, media monitoring means)?
E. Have health workers been trained in surveillance objectives and procedures? Is there supportive supervision?
F. Do communication channels in the national system allow immediate reporting of any suspected disease or event, including unknown morbidity and mortality, clusters of disease or syndrome cases, or unusual or unexpected disease patterns?
G. Can immediate reporting be done through basic (like mobile text messages) or more advanced electronic health information systems (like DHIS2)? Who can access these applications and devices?
H. Is there evidence of rapid occurrence of epidemic-prone diseases and acute public health events?
I. Are there standard operating procedures to indicate what information should be reported at what frequency? Detection and reporting?

5.3.4 Early Warning Management

A. Does the surveillance system have early warning and epidemic thresholds to detect suspected outbreaks? Is there evidence that it has been effectively used?
B. Does the monitoring system include an alert log that records all signals, events, and alerts? (A signal log is used to record the occurrence and response of all signals.)
C. Are signals, events, and alerts managed according to agreed standardized workflows?
D. Are there SOPs to validate and risk assess incoming reports?

5.3.5 Outbreak Response

A. For each confirmed alert, what are the corresponding response activities according to the SOP?
B. In the event of a confirmed outbreak, has the surveillance system updated the case investigation forms for each key disease?
C. Does the surveillance system have standard operating procedures for notifying and investigating cases during an outbreak?
D. Is there a mechanism to strengthen surveillance during an outbreak through the surveillance system, such as by actively finding cases or tracing contacts?

E. Is there evidence of the ability to rapidly investigate and respond to outbreaks (i.e., regional level RRTs available for public health event response or support from non-governmental organizations)?
F. Is there a systematic performance monitoring and evaluation system?

5.3.6 *Data Analysis and Sharing*

A. Does the surveillance system regularly allow the analysis and sharing of surveillance data using standardized information products (e.g., weekly or monthly epidemiological bulletins, charts, maps)?
B. Are data protection operations in place?

5.3.7 *Infrastructure*

A. Are there minimum human resources at the crisis level (district/provincial/national), including healthcare personnel for case detection, data collection and analysis, and outbreak investigation and response?
B. What are the gaps in human resources?
C. Are existing electronic tools available for data collection, analysis, and rapid dissemination of information?

5.3.8 *Coordination*

A. Is there a trained EWAR coordinator and pre-identified coordination center (at the regional and provincial/state level) at least in the initial stage?
B. Is there a partner list of existing government and non-governmental organization partners who provide patient care and can serve as reporting sites (e.g., health facilities operating health facilities and national and international non-governmental organizations)?
C. Is there a list of fixed and mobile laboratories?
D. Are there dedicated transportation means for EWAR (like motorcycles or vehicles)?

5.4 Evaluation of the Effectiveness of Public Health Emergency Decision-Making

Continuous and consistent monitoring of system performance is key to ensuring the effective operation of EWAR to enhance early warning capabilities. Structured assessments will help key stakeholders understand whether activities have produced the initially envisioned results/changes (Cai 2021).

Assessments are cyclical activities that focus more on outcomes and impacts. They may also more broadly concern systemic issues such as policy, legislative coordination, cooperation, partnerships, funding, labor, supply and equipment, community participation and empowerment. Personnel responsible for regular EWAR assessments are typically suggested to be external to the implementation team to ensure objectivity, but assessments can also be conducted in collaboration with implementation team members. In terms of funding, scope, staff, and time, evaluations require significant resources. Although it should be planned at the design stage of EWAR, it is not advisable to implement evaluations immediately during the establishment and functioning of EWAR.

In addition to the monitoring and evaluation described in this chapter, it is important to clearly establish and communicate feedback mechanisms for stakeholders; for example, email addresses, forums, or other contact methods, where EWAR stakeholders can provide feedback or raise any issues related to EWAR.

5.4.1 Monitoring EWAR Performance

The execution of EWAR must be regularly monitored at all levels (from national to sub-national levels, sub-national to health facilities, and health facilities to community levels) to ensure proper functioning and identify any potential difficulties. Monitoring of EWAR should be integrated from the start; the application of performance indicators (Table 5.2) as well as the frequency and methods of collection should be clearly included in the implementation plan and standard operating procedures (ECDC 2019). EWAR contact points at all levels must have a clear understanding of how to monitor the system, what specific activities need to be implemented at each level, and the expected EWAR performance standards and key performance indicators. EWAR contact points should also understand how to assess the data quality of the collected indicators. If there are any changes in the indicators, the EWAR coordination center should ensure that all reporting sites are aware and make adjustments. The availability of the data itself greatly facilitates the monitoring of EWAR; for example, based on the data flow/existing data at the health facility level, it is easy to assess the completeness of surveillance reporting as well as the consistency and timeliness of weekly reporting by health facilities.

Targets can be set for each attribute to help measure performance levels. When setting targets, it's important to remember the context applicability of the targets

Table 5.2 EWAR key monitoring indicators

Attribute	Indicator/element	Frequency	Numerator	Denominator
Completeness	Completeness of reporting	Weekly	Number of reporting sites that reported (including zero reporting) in a given week	Number of reporting sites in EWAR
Timeliness	Percentage of sites submitting reports on time	Weekly	Number of total reporting sites submitting a report in a given week by the stated deadline	Number of total reporting sites submitting a report in a given week before or after the deadline
	Number of EBS signals reported on time	Weekly	Number of new EBS signals reported within a specified timeframe after detection (48 h)	–
	Proportion of signals verified within 48 h	Weekly	Number of new signals verified within a specified timeframe (48 h)	Number of new signals reported in the same week
	Proportion of outbreak investigations initiated within 72 h after verification	Weekly	Number of outbreak investigations initiated within a specified timeframe (72 h) after verification	Number of outbreaks verified in the same week
	Number and proportion of suspected outbreaks that were laboratory-confirmed within 72 h	Monthly	Number of suspected outbreaks that were laboratory confirmed within 72 h	Number of suspected outbreaks in the same week
	Proportion of events risk assessed and investigated within 48 h after verification	Monthly	Number of new verified events that are risk assessed and investigated within a specified timeframe (48 h)	Number of new events verified in the same week
Data quality	Proportion of reporting sites receiving routine supervision visits	Monthly	Number of reporting sites receiving a routine supervision visit in a given month compared to a set threshold	Number of reporting sites

and the importance of monitoring trends over time to get indicators of EWAR's performance.

5.4.2 *EWAR Performance Evaluation*

Regular evaluations of EWAR should combine quantitative and qualitative methods, ensuring meaningful community participation and involvement. More specifically, evaluations should assess community ownership of the system and whether communities are empowered with the tools, skills, and resources to lead community-based public health functions and the provision of health services, particularly for vulnerable and hard-to-reach populations.

The evaluation includes an assessment of the attributes of the surveillance system (Table 5.3) (ECDC 2019). At the very least, the evaluation should address the most important attributes in a specific context. The assessment of each attribute provides evidence of which elements of EWAR are functioning well and which can be strengthened.

The evaluation should also include an assessment of the dissemination and communication of EWAR information, looking at the completeness, timeliness, and predictability of the dissemination. For example, are stakeholders receiving the information; do they understand it? How are they using this information; is it being released in a consistent manner, on the same day each week; are these changes clearly communicated to the target audience?

Furthermore, EWAR evaluations should look at broader systemic issues, such as establishing relevant policies, legislation, coordination mechanisms, funding, sufficient labor, and supplies for EWAR in emergencies.

5.4.2.1 Timing of Evaluation

The timing of regular EWAR evaluations depends on the context, feasibility, and duration of the emergency. An initial evaluation should be conducted after EWAR is set up and running. Once suggestions from the first evaluation are incorporated, a second evaluation is recommended to assess improvements. If the emergency remains relatively stable and regular monitoring indicates good functioning of EWAR, subsequent evaluations can be conducted at different time intervals based on feasibility and need. If the underlying emergency is unstable, evaluations should be conducted according to fluctuations in the situation. An evaluation can be initiated after any significant changes in the system, regardless of the type of emergency, including:

A. system stabilization—reporting locations remain stable;
B. system expansion—increasing reporting locations, introducing or strengthening electronic detection systems, introducing hotlines, increasing laboratory testing capabilities or introducing rapid diagnostic techniques;

Table 5.3 Key indicators by attribute

Attribute	Indicator
Simplicity	• EWAR integration with other systems • Method to collect, manage, enter, analyse and disseminate data • Time spent on maintaining the system • Amount and type of data collected for each priority disease
Flexibility	• Process to add/remove health units/partners • Retrospective review of how system responded to a new demand, such as: • Emerging health events • Changes in case definitions • Variations in funding
Data quality	• Quality control practices • Critical discussion of data and reports with partners • Use of standardized tools and forms • Staff who can correctly identify immediately notifiable diseases • Staff who accurately provide case definitions • Staff who accurately provide alert thresholds • Staff who can correctly explain the alert notification procedure • Training: • Current EWAR health facility staff trained in EWAR • New EWAR partners/reporting sources (added within the past six months) trained in EWAR • Length of training courses (initial and refresher) • Supervision and feedback: • Health facilities which received feedback in the past X period • Health facilities which received supervisory visits in the past X period • Legibility of forms and registers • Completeness of forms and registers • Application of case definition based on observation (if feasible) • Regularity of reporting sites
Acceptability	• Barriers to reporting • Organization/agency/staff willingness to participate • Perceived strengths and weaknesses of the system • Support and feedback to EWAR staff • Regular meetings to review EWAR (e.g., strengthen practices, discuss progress, feedback) • Responsiveness of the system to suggestions or comments
Representativeness	• Groups or subgroups not covered by or included in the system • Systematic exclusion or barriers to healthcare access
Stability	• Interruptions to reporting and impact on the system • Costs involved to maintain the system • Staff turnover • Uninterrupted weeks with functioning health facilities in the last X period

(continued)

Table 5.3 (continued)

Attribute	Indicator
Usefulness	• Perceived usefulness of EWAR data and bulletins • Public health action (e.g., control measures implemented) based on EWAR data • System's ability to meet its objectives
Sensitivity	• Of mode of detection • By disease, if feasible
Predictive value positive	• Overall • By disease, if feasible
Timeliness	• Time from signal notification to verification • Time from signal verification to investigation • Time from investigation to receipt of results • Time from verification to implementation of control measures • Sites reporting by the weekly deadline

C. adoption of new reporting tools, formats or new technologies (including digital systems);
D. integration with other surveillance systems or transition to regular surveillance systems.

5.4.2.2 Evaluators

To ensure objectivity, it is recommended that evaluators be external to the implementation team, but evaluations can also be conducted in collaboration with members of the implementation team.

The number of evaluators may vary depending on the environment, scale of implementation, and availability. However, in all formal evaluations, at least two evaluators should be involved. Those responsible for EWAR evaluation need to have the following characteristics.

A. They have not been directly involved in the implementation of the EWAR system under consideration.
B. There is a balance of institutional representation; for instance, they ensure the participation of different stakeholders, including national public health institutes, health departments, WHO, Global Outbreak Alert and Response Network, NGOs, academic institutions or independent consultants.
C. They bring a multidisciplinary set of skills and expertise. Depending on the scope and type of the emergency, the evaluation team can include experts from laboratory, clinical, epidemiological, health systems, social and behavioral sciences, veterinary and/or WASH project backgrounds.
D. They have received formal training and/or have experience in conducting EWAR evaluations according to standardized evaluation guidelines.

E. They are able to speak the local language to enable qualitative data collection components. If evaluators are unable to join the team in the local language, an alternative is to use local community liaisons.

If an evaluation is conducted by a single evaluator, it is crucial that the evaluation results are interpreted by a larger representative group of stakeholders involved in EWAR. This ensures that evaluation results are interpreted in a context-appropriate and constructive manner, and that the recommendations identified are feasible.

5.4.2.3 Evaluation Method

Standardized tools should be used to evaluate EWAR in emergencies, with adjustments made as necessary based on local conditions. Where appropriate, all tools, templates, and questionnaires should also be translated into the local language.

To fully understand the functionality of EWAR, determining the appropriate method is key. Quantitative and qualitative methods should be used in a complementary manner. For example, the sensitivity of the system is evaluated using quantitative data, while qualitative methods are more suitable than quantitative methods when evaluating the acceptability of EWAR.

The WHO Eastern Mediterranean Regional Office and the US Centers for Disease Control and Prevention have developed the "Early Warning, Alert and Response Network for Outbreaks: 2017 Evaluation Scheme". This is a standardized tool that can be used for evaluation in emergencies. This scheme establishes standard practices for evaluating EWAR systems, focusing on common challenges faced in the implementation, operation, and termination of EWAR in emergencies, and challenges faced in the evaluation itself. In addition, it provides standard templates and questionnaires for data collection and data analysis matrices linked to indicators, and special considerations for remote evaluations when physical access is limited.

5.4.2.4 Dissemination of Evaluation Results

When drafting an evaluation plan, a plan for disseminating the survey results should be developed, listing all anticipated users. The anticipated users and dissemination methods of the research results depend on the environment. Anticipated users may include:

A. Ministries of Health, Agriculture/Forestry and other departments considered relevant;
B. Those involved in the implementation of EWAR (e.g., stakeholders at the community level, health facility level, sub-national and national levels involved in surveillance, national public health authorities, national health research institutes, NGOs, WHO, health clusters, WASH project teams, nutrition clusters and other inter-sectoral groups);
C. Stakeholders involved in response activities;

D. Donors;
E. Other surveillance stakeholders, who may also come from other sectors on a discretionary basis; and
F. A wider community/population within the surveillance scope.

After the evaluation is completed, it is recommended to hold a meeting with the aforementioned anticipated users. The meeting should specifically share and discuss survey results, identified recommendations and their implementation in layman and non-technical language. In addition, evaluation results can be shared through summary documents/reports, oral presentations at health sector meetings and formal consultation meetings. These should particularly consider different administrative regions outside the central location. To ensure feedback to those who collected the data, dissemination efforts should specifically target reporting locations and community-based information providers. This may require the preparation of appropriate dissemination materials and translation into the local language. The release of research results does not end the EWAR evaluation process. It should lay the foundation for stakeholder commitment to implementing evaluation recommendations.

5.4.2.5 Implementation of Recommendations

The execution of recommendations is a crucial step in the evaluation process. A core group should be established to monitor the execution of each recommendation. An action plan with a clear timetable should be developed to complete the recommended improvements and corrections, including omissions. Some recommendations may require process adjustments, capacity building improvements, and information sharing and response, while others may include adopting new ways of working, such as introducing new technologies (Hethcote 2000). Adequate resources should be mobilized according to the nature of the recommendations to fund institutional reforms. After successful implementation of the recommendations, the core group should decide on the next evaluation cycle to obtain system enhancement attributes after the recommendations.

References

Cai Y (2021) The criteria for global public health security capacity assessment: Implications from China's practices for fighting COVID-19. Chin Public Adm 6:145–154

European Centre for Disease Prevention and Control (ECDC) (2019) Operational tool on rapid risk assessment methodology. https://www.ecdc.europa.eu/en/publications-data/operational-tool-rapid-risk-assessment-methodology-ecdc-2019

Hethcote, HW (2000) The mathematics of infectious diseases. SIAM Rev

Part II
Practices of Risk Management in Public Health

Chapter 6
Practice of Risk Management on COVID-19

COVID-19 is the disease caused by the SARS-CoV-2 coronavirus. The epidemic of SARS-CoV-2 is a major global public health problem. It usually spreads between people in close contact. Most people make a full recovery without needing hospital treatment. People with severe symptoms should seek medical care as soon as possible. COVID-19 Pandemic was recognized as Public Health Emergency of International Concern (PHEIC) by the WHO from January 30, 2020 to May 5, 2023. COVID-19 vaccines provide strong protection against severe illness and death. Although a person can still get COVID-19 after vaccination, they are more likely to have mild or no symptoms. Anyone can get sick with COVID-19 and become seriously ill or die, but most people will recover without treatment. People over age 60 and those with existing medical conditions have a higher risk of getting seriously ill. These conditions include high blood pressure, diabetes, obesity, immunosuppression including HIV, cancer and pregnancy. Unvaccinated people also have a higher risk of severe symptoms.

6.1 Disease Burden

6.1.1 Burden of Disease

COVID-19 has caused a significant global disease burden. According to data from the World Health Organization, as of April 2024, over 770 million confirmed cases and over 7.04 million deaths have been reported worldwide, affecting more than 232 countries and regions. In terms of regional distribution, among the six regions of the WHO, the number of confirmed cases are as follows: Europe 279 million, Western Pacific 208 million, Americas 193 million, Southeast Asia 61.29 million, Eastern Mediterranean 23.42 million, Africa 9.58 million; The number of deaths

J. Liu, *Risk Management in Public Health*, Innovation in Risk Analysis,
https://doi.org/10.1007/978-981-97-6826-4_6

are: Americas 3.02 million, Europe 2.27 million, Southeast Asia 809,000, Western Pacific 421,000, Eastern Mediterranean 352,000, Africa 176,000.

6.1.2 Loss of Life

Global all-cause mortality followed two distinct patterns over the 2020–2021 as COVID-19 pandemic: age-standardised mortality rates declined between 1950 and 2019 (a 62.8% [95% UI 60.5–65.1] decline), and increased during the COVID-19 pandemic period (2020–2021; 5.1% [0.9–9.6] increase). In contrast with the overall reverse in mortality trends during the pandemic period, child mortality continued to decline, with 4.66 million (3.98–5.50) global deaths in children younger than 5 years in 2021 compared with 5.21 million (4.50–6.01) in 2019. An estimated 131 million (126–137) people died globally from all causes in 2020 and 2021 combined, of which 15.9 million (14.7–17.2) were due to the COVID-19 pandemic (measured by excess mortality, which includes deaths directly due to SARS-CoV-2 infection and those indirectly due to other social, economic, or behavioral changes associated with the pandemic). Excess mortality rates exceeded 150 deaths per 100 000 population during at least one year of the pandemic in 80 countries and territories, whereas 20 nations had a negative excess mortality rate in 2020 or 2021, indicating that all-cause mortality in these countries was lower during the pandemic than expected based on historical trends. Between 1950 and 2021, global life expectancy at birth increased by 22.7 years (20.8–24.8), from 49.0 years (46.7–51.3) to 71.7 years (70.9–72.5). Global life expectancy at birth declined by 1.6 years (1.0–2.2) between 2019 and 2021, reversing historical trends. An increase in life expectancy was only observed in 32 (15.7%) of 204 countries and territories between 2019 and 2021. The global population reached 7.89 billion (7.67–8.13) people in 2021, by which time 56 of 204 countries and territories had peaked and subsequently populations have declined. The largest proportion of population growth between 2020 and 2021 was in sub-Saharan Africa (39.5% [28.4–52.7]) and south Asia (26.3% [9.0–44.7]). From 2000 to 2021, the ratio of the population aged 65 years and older to the population aged younger than 15 years increased in 188 (92.2%) of 204 nations (GBD 2021 Demographics Collaborators 2024).

Global adult mortality rates markedly increased during the COVID-19 pandemic in 2020 and 2021, reversing past decreasing trends, while child mortality rates continued to decline, albeit more slowly than in earlier years. Although COVID-19 had a substantial impact on many demographic indicators during the first 2 years of the pandemic, overall global health progress over the 72 years evaluated has been profound, with considerable improvements in mortality and life expectancy. Additionally, we observed a deceleration of global population growth since 2017, despite steady or increasing growth in lower-income countries, combined with a continued global shift of population age structures towards older ages. These demographic changes will likely present future challenges to health systems, economies, and societies (GBD 2021 Demographics Collaborators 2024).

6.1.3 *The Worldwide Economic Impact of the COVID-19 Shocks*

In the macroeconomic impact at early stage, the COVID-19 shock propagated quickly across countries causing a synchronized negative impact. More than 90% of the global economy experienced a contraction in per capita GDP, the highest share of countries simultaneously contracting since the Great Depression of 1930–1932 (World Bank Global Outlook 2020). The shock propagated through three key channels: (i) a disruption of global value chains, (ii) restrictions to international mobility, which affected economies and activities differently, depending on their exposure and preparedness; and (iii) a reduction in cross-country remittances. Trade experienced a short-lived but deep dive. Goods trade fell rapidly, adding to the economic decline in manufacturing countries, but recovered quickly, reflecting the substitution of demand from contact-intensive services (impaired by COVID-related restriction) to goods, and the considerable resilience of global value chains to transitory disruptions in the first semester (The World Bank 2021).

In 2020, it severely impacted output growth and employment, particularly in middle-income countries. Governments responded primarily by increasing expenditure, supported by an expansion of the supply of money and debt. These policies did not put upward pressure on prices until 2021. International trade was severely disrupted across all regions in 2020 but subsequently recovered. For 2021, the adverse effects of the COVID-19 shock on output and prices were significant and persistent, especially in emerging and developing countries (Martin et al. 2023).

6.2 Risk Assessment

The emergence of the COVID-19 has had a severe impact globally. The following risk assessment issues need to be noted from a societal and individual perspective, respectively.

6.2.1 *Societal Risk Assessment for COVID-19*

To effectively prevent and control this global health crisis, a comprehensive risk assessment is crucial. COVID-19 risk assessment mainly involves the following six aspects:

6.2.1.1 Epidemic Situation and Transmission Risk

The assessment of transmission risk mainly identifies the transmission routes and speed of the coronavirus, and determines the most susceptible populations. It requires information on virus mutation, confirmed case numbers, and mortality rates. These data can help us understand the severity of the epidemic, predict possible development paths, and formulate and implement corresponding prevention and control strategies in advance.

6.2.1.2 Susceptibility and Health Risk of Populations

This part mainly considers the structural characteristics of the population, such as age and gender, as well as the health status of the population, such as the presence of chronic diseases. These factors may increase or decrease the risk of an individual being infected with the coronavirus. For example, the elderly and those with underlying diseases are more likely to have severe symptoms. The assessment of health risks focuses on the impact of the COVID-19 epidemic on public health, including morbidity and mortality. Understanding susceptibility helps us carry out more targeted health education and vaccination prevention measures.

6.2.1.3 Hygiene Environment

It includes the survival ability of the virus in different environments, such as public places, workplaces, and home environments. This is crucial for judging the risk of virus transmission and formulating appropriate hygiene and cleaning measures.

6.2.1.4 Prevention and Control Measures

Prevention and control measures assessment checks the effectiveness of our prevention and control measures. It includes the effectiveness of health education, the coverage of vaccination, the awareness of prevention and control among residents, and the capacity of medical equipment and treatment. By evaluating the implementation of these measures, we can know where we are doing well and where we need to improve, and adjust strategies accordingly.

6.2.1.5 Socio-Economic Impact

The assessment of socio-economic impact mainly considers the impact of the epidemic on economic development, the job market, and even social order. The impact of the COVID-19 epidemic on the global, national, regional, and individual economy, including losses in production, employment, income, and supply chains.

Many industries have stopped production, people are unemployed, and the global economy has suffered a significant blow. The assessment of supply chain risk mainly determines the vulnerability of the global supply chain, including the supply of food, medical equipment, and other necessary items. Understanding these impacts can provide direction for economic recovery planning.

6.2.1.6 Psychological Stress Impact

We cannot deny that both the epidemic itself and the preventive measures have had an impact on people's mental health. Fear, anxiety, depression, and other negative psychological states are intensifying. Social risk assessment mainly analyzes the impact of the novel coronavirus epidemic on social mental health, community relations, education, and the quality of life of residents. This helps understand public needs, find solutions, and alleviate the negative impact of the epidemic on communities and individuals.

6.2.2 Individual Risk Assessment for COVID-19

The individual health level assessment of COVID-19 risk typically involves the following aspects:

6.2.2.1 Individual Health Status Assessment

Evaluates the individual's basic health condition, including factors such as age, gender, and existing chronic diseases. These factors may increase the risk of COVID-19 infection or the severity of the disease. For example, patients with underlying diseases such as heart disease, diabetes, lung disease, and the elderly have a higher risk of severe illness and death compared to other populations.

6.2.2.2 Lifestyle Habits Control

Understanding a person's lifestyle habits, such as diet, sleep, and exercise, can impact an individual's health status and ability to resist COVID-19. A balanced diet, regular sleep schedule, and moderate exercise can help boost the body's immunity.

6.2.2.3 Medical History and Contact History Review

Assess the individual's recent medical history and patient contact history, especially for hospital treatments, contact with COVID-19 infected or suspected infected individuals. These situations may expose the individual to a higher risk of infection for a certain period.

6.2.2.4 Implementation of Preventive Measures

Measure the implementation of preventive measures in daily life, such as whether masks are worn correctly, maintaining social distance, avoiding overcrowding, washing hands in time, etc. These are important steps to reduce the risk of COVID-19 infection.

6.2.2.5 Vaccine Inoculation Status Check

Understand whether the individual has been vaccinated with the COVID-19 vaccine, which vaccine they have received, and whether they have completed all scheduled doses. Vaccination is currently one of the most effective measures to prevent and control COVID-19.

These are mainly about the individual-level COVID-19 risk assessment. Through such assessment, one can more accurately judge a person's risk of infection, which is very helpful for formulating individualized protective measures and treatment strategies.

6.3 Surveillance and Early Warning

Global COVID-19 early warning and monitoring is a complex and intricate process that involves the following aspects:

A. Case Monitoring and Epidemiological Investigation: Early detection and rapid response to potential outbreaks of COVID-19 through the collection and analysis of test results for the coronavirus. This includes tracking known cases and screening potential infected person. By collecting information about the mode, rhythm, and extent of disease transmission, the development trend of the epidemic can be analyzed and predicted.
B. Contact Tracing and Isolation: By tracing contacts of cases and setting appropriate isolation measures, further spread of the epidemic can be prevented.
C. Health Status Monitoring: Collect data on individual health conditions, such as vaccination status, underlying disease conditions, etc., to assess the risk of comorbidities, complications, or severe illness.

D. Healthcare System Capability Assessment: Evaluate the handling capacity of the healthcare system, including supply of beds, human resources, facilities, equipment, and vaccine stockpiles, etc.
E. Application of Big Data in Early Warning Monitoring: Predict and warn of epidemic trends by collecting and analyzing data from various sources, including social media, medical health applications, etc.
F. International Cooperation and Reporting: Includes sharing information with the World Health Organization and other national health departments to keep abreast of global epidemic dynamics and make timely response measures. Combining all of the above aspects can provide policymakers and the public with comprehensive information about the COVID-19 epidemic, thereby making timely and effective prevention and control decisions.

This section provides a brief introduction using the COVID-19 monitoring system established by China as an example.

6.3.1 Routine Monitoring

6.3.1.1 Virus Mutation Monitoring

Representative cities' sentinel hospitals' emergency department cases, severe and fatal cases, and representative port (including land, air, and sea ports) entry personnel's positive samples of coronavirus nucleic acid test are selected to carry out full genome sequencing of the coronavirus, and the sequences are promptly reported to the China CDC. Real-time understanding of virus strain mutation trends, timely capture of new mutant strains, and analysis of the impact of mutations on virus characteristics, immune escape ability, etc.

6.3.1.2 Case Reporting

All levels and types of medical institutions should timely report cases of novel coronavirus infection in accordance with laws and regulations, implement relevant information reporting management requirements, and report confirmed cases of novel coronavirus and asymptomatic infections online within 24 h through the China Disease Prevention and Control Information System after diagnosis. For discovered severe, critical, fatal cases and other special cases, disease control institutions should promptly carry out epidemiological investigations and upload related epidemiological reports as required.

6.3.1.3 Sentinel Hospital Monitoring

Based on the national influenza surveillance network, monitoring of the coronavirus is carried out on influenza-like illnesses (ILI) and inpatient severe acute respiratory infections (SARI) in 554 national influenza surveillance sentinel hospitals.

6.3.1.4 Unexplained Pneumonia Monitoring

All levels and types of medical institutions nationwide should do a good job in the discovery and reporting of unexplained pneumonia cases in accordance with the requirements of the "National Unexplained Pneumonia Case Surveillance, Investigation and Management Plan".

6.3.1.5 Sewage Monitoring

Regions with conditions can carry out monitoring of the coronavirus in sewage, dynamically evaluate the epidemic intensity, change trend and virus mutation situation of novel coronavirus infection.

6.3.2 Emergency Monitoring

Emergency monitoring refers to the monitoring measures carried out during the epidemic period based on routine monitoring.

6.3.2.1 Nucleic Acid and Antigen Testing Monitoring

All regions should use the local coronavirus nucleic acid testing information system and residents' self-testing antigen information collection channels (platforms) to collect and report the number of nucleic acid tests and residents' self-antigen tests and the number of positives every day, and dynamically analyze the infection and disease situation of the population.

6.3.2.2 Fever Clinic (Room) Monitoring in Medical Institutions

All regions should count the number of visits, nucleic acid and antigen tests, and the number of positives in fever clinics (rooms) of all levels and types of medical institutions every day, and report them at all levels. Dynamically analyze the changes in the number of visits and infection rate in fever clinics (rooms).

6.3.2.3 Key Institution Monitoring

All regions should carry out epidemic monitoring in elderly care institutions and social welfare institutions within their jurisdiction, carry out health monitoring, regular antigen testing or nucleic acid testing on the cared-for persons and staff in the institutions, and dynamically analyze the infection change trend of the staff in elderly care institutions and social welfare institutions.

6.3.2.4 Student Monitoring

All regions can carry out daily fever, dry cough and other novel coronavirus infection symptom monitoring for middle and primary school students in school, and carry out antigen or nucleic acid testing as needed, and dynamically analyze the infection change trend of middle and primary school students.

6.3.2.5 Community Population Sentinel Monitoring

All regions can formulate a community population novel coronavirus infection sentinel monitoring plan in combination with reality, understand the occurrence of related clinical symptoms and medical behavior of residents, and dynamically grasp the level of new infections and cumulative infections in the population.

6.3.3 Monitoring Information Analysis and Reporting

Disease prevention and control institutions dynamically analyze the changes in the trends of infectors, especially severe, critical, and fatal cases. When an abnormal increase in infections is found, infectors are distributed in clusters, or severe, critical, and fatal cases occur, they should promptly verify and report to the same level of health administrative department and the superior disease prevention and control institution, and regularly notify the lower level disease prevention and control institution and medical institution of the epidemic analysis information. According to the needs of prevention and control, timely release warning information to the society.

6.3.4 Epidemic Information Release

Release epidemic information in a timely manner according to the development of the epidemic and the needs of prevention and control. Hold press conferences as needed, organize experts in relevant fields, clarify doubts through media interviews, etc., popularize protective knowledge, and respond to hot issues in a timely manner.

6.4 Prevention and Control Strategy and Measures

COVID-19, as one of the infectious diseases affecting the majority of countries globally since the twenty-first century, has seen varying control strategies implemented by different countries during pandemic, leading to diverse outcomes in managing the spread. Summarizing diverse preventive and control measures is conducive to better addressing the challenges posed by globally prevalent infectious diseases.

6.4.1 Prevention and Control Strategy

During the COVID-19 pandemic, three goals corresponding to five strategies were presented control COVID-19 pandemic including no community transmission (exclusion and elimination), controlled transmission (suppression and mitigation), or uncontrolled transmission across different countries (Table 6.1) (Baker et al. 2020, 2023). It is noted that choosing a strategy is not necessarily a fixed path, and countries might change their approach. Of five strategies, elimination of community transmission offers public health, equity, and potentially economic advantages compared with a control strategy using mitigation or suppression (Baker et al. 2020). Baker et al. proposed that elimination might be the preferred strategy for responding to new emerging infectious diseases with pandemic potential and moderate to high severity, particularly while key parameters are being estimated (2020). However, Baker et al. emphasized five experiences of covid-19 pandemic using elimination strategy (Baker et al. 2020). Firstly, elimination is more likely to be achieved quickly with informed scientific input, strong political commitment, and decisive action. Secondly, investment in three broad categories of public health infrastructure is needed to achieve elimination or quickly regain it in the event of an outbreak: border management with closely supervised quarantine of all arrivals from places that have not eliminated the virus; case based control measures, notably testing, case isolation, contact tracing, and quarantine; and population based interventions such as physical distancing and mask use. Thirdly, outbreaks arising from border control failures might occur after elimination has been achieved and these require swift and decisive action. Finally, given the inevitable loss of employment and other social disruption when stringent lockdowns are used, a range of health, social, and economic support measures are likely to be required.

Table 6.1 Strategic choices for responding to covid-19 and other pandemics

Type	Characteristic	Period	Countries	Other diseases
Exclusion (eradication) strategy	Maximum action to exclude disease/ International cooperation allows interventions to reduce transmission to zero permanently at the global level	Return to carefully managed "new normal" (within 2–3 months) Requires persisting quarantine at borders until effective vaccine and/ or antimicrobial interventions	e.g, some Pacific Island countries and territories	e.g, smallpox
Elimination strategy	Maximum action to exclude disease and eliminate community transmission/ High disease burden and feasibility justify interventions to reduce transmission to zero for a defined geographical area and time period	The same as exclusion strategy	e.g, mainland China, New Zealand	e.g, measles and poliomyelitis
Suppression strategy	Action increased in stepwise and targeted manner to substantially lower case numbers and outbreaks/ High disease burden justifies interventions to reduce impact but elimination not sufficiently feasible and desirable	Prolonged control measures until effective vaccine and/ or antimicrobial interventions (12–18 + months) or switch strategy, which aim to minimize disease burden	e.g, most countries in Europe and North America	e.g, tuberculosis and HIV/AIDS
Mitigation strategy	Action taken to flatten the peak' to avoid overwhelming health services and protect the most vulnerable / High disease burden justifies interventions to reduce impact but elimination not sufficiently feasible and desirable	Pandemic spreads through population until "herd immunity" and/or effective vaccine and/or antimicrobial interventions (12–18 + months) or switch strategy, which aim to avoid overwhelming the health-care system	e.g, Sweden (at least initially)	e.g, pandemic infuenza
No substantive strategy	Largely uncontrolled pandemic wave / Low disease burden, or lack of feasible interventions, resources, or political will to act	The same as mitigation strategy	e.g, some lower income countries	NA

6.4.2 *Prevention and Control Measures*

6.4.2.1 Control of the Source of Infection

During the COVID-19 pandemic, controlling the source of infection, including individuals infected with SARS-Cov-2 and asymptomatic cases, was of paramount importance, particularly in the early stages of the outbreak when the modes of transmission were not fully understood and effective vaccines were not yet available. Early detection of SARS-Cov-2 was crucial for understanding the spread of the pandemic and formulating appropriate responses, aiding in the reduction of disease transmission, management of cases, and contact tracing. Implementing large-scale testing allowed for the early identification and isolation of COVID-19 cases, along with strict intervention for confirmed cases and close contacts. South Korea leveraged its experience from the 2015 Middle East Respiratory Syndrome (MERS) outbreak, with the government collaborating with the private sector to develop COVID-19 test kits even before the first case was confirmed in the country. Concurrently, it swiftly established facilities for mass nucleic acid testing, such as K-Walk-Thru and Drive-thru testing stations, enabling the rapid and safe collection of samples for nucleic acid testing and enhancing daily testing capacity. Following the identification of multiple confirmed cases among foreign workers in April 2020, Singapore initiated extensive testing, isolation, and treatment for the young migrant worker population. The Australian government allocated over 750 million AUD to improve nucleic acid testing capabilities, making it one of the leading countries in tests per thousand people during the initial months of the outbreak. Consequently, these countries witnessed a decline in daily new cases following the intensification of testing efforts, achieving preliminary control over the pandemic before the emergence of the Delta variant.

6.4.2.2 Interrupting the Mode of Transmission

In response to the pandemic, countries have implemented a series of stringent policies, including "lockdowns", closure of schools and workplaces, cancellation of events and public gatherings, and restrictions on public transportation. The aim of these measures is to mitigate the spread by decreasing physical distancing between population. Australia, South Korea, and Singapore implemented strict policies early in the outbreak and had largely controlled the situation by April 2020. However, as control measures were further relaxed, including mask mandates, contact tracing, and domestic travel restrictions, resurgences occurred. Israel, after achieving initial control of the outbreak and with the continuous increase in vaccine coverage, let down its guard against prevention and rapidly eased non-pharmaceutical interventions (NPIs), leading to a worsening of the pandemic. Subsequently, tightening control measures again, it fell into a cycle of "severe outbreak—national and city lockdowns—outbreak mitigation—lifting of measures—severe outbreak." India adopted a prolonged national lockdown strategy in the early stages of outbreak control, with its Oxford Stringency Index consistently between 80 and 100. This strategy only temporarily curbed the growth in the number of cases, which was related to the implementation of the policies. Despite high stringency, large-scale election campaigns and gatherings were still held. To adapt to the situation of scarce medical resources, high population density, and a significant impoverished population, India introduced a train makeshift hospital plan, drawing on China's experience with mobile cabin hospitals, establishing temporary isolation beds. However, as lockdown measures were relaxed, domestic travel restrictions were lifted, and millions of stranded migrant workers left the industrialized western regions for rural areas in the north and east. Coupled with a clear insufficiency in testing capacity, the rampant domestic Delta variant, and the holding of large religious activities, the second wave became more severe than the first, making it the first country to report over 400,000 new cases within 24 h. Furthermore, to reduce the risk of infection for individuals during the COVID-19 pandemic, individuals can wear masks, wash hands frequently, and maintain safe social distances in public places. People from areas of moderate to high risk should cancel travel plans, and those from other areas should postpone travel to areas of moderate to high risk, to reduce population mobility.

6.4.2.3 Protecting Susceptible Populations

At present, vaccination stands out as a cost-effective method for protecting susceptible populations (Du et al. 2021; Liu et al. 2022). COVID-19 vaccines have demonstrated effective prevention and protection against the original strain and the Alpha variant, which was predominant in early 2021. Despite this, incomplete vaccine coverage in the early stages of the pandemic, coupled with ongoing community transmission, has facilitated the emergence of new variants. The efficacy of early vaccines against these variants is somewhat reduced, and over time, the protective power of the vaccines can decay to some extent. Consequently, countries continue to develop vaccines targeted at these variants.

6.4.2.4 Other Non-Pharmaceutical Intervention Measures

NPIs are public health measures aimed at reducing transmission through decreased contact rates. In the absence of vaccines and therapeutic treatments in the early stages of the pandemic, NPIs were crucial in managing the outbreak. As evidenced by the case of South Korea, robust testing capabilities and advanced healthcare facilities are key to controlling the spread of the novel coronavirus. Singapore implemented comprehensive and stringent control measures, including extensive testing, contact tracing, international travel restrictions, closure of public transportation, mask-wearing mandates, workplace closures, and cancellation of public events, which proved effective in the initial stages of the pandemic. Therefore, epidemic control should employ a multifaceted approach, devising a comprehensive and systematic strategy to effectively fortify the barriers against the spread of the disease.

References

Baker MG, Durrheim D, Hsu LY, Wilson N (2023) COVID-19 and other pandemics require a coherent response strategy. Lancet 401(10373):265–266

Baker MG, Wilson N, Blakely T (2020) Elimination could be the optimal response strategy for covid-19 and other emerging pandemic diseases. BMJ (Clinical research ed):m4907

Du M, Liu M, Liu J (2021) Progress in research of epidemiologic feature and control of SARS-CoV-2 Delta variant. Chin J Epidemiol 42(10):1774–1779

GBD 2021 Demographics Collaborators (2024) Global age-sex-specific mortality, life expectancy, and population estimates in 204 countries and territories and 811 subnational locations, 1950–2021, and the impact of the COVID-19 pandemic: a comprehensive demographic analysis for the Global Burden of Disease Study 2021. Lancet 403(10440):1989–2056

Liu Q, Du M, Liu J, Liu M (2022) Long COVID-19 and its scientific prevention and control. Chin J Dis Control Prev 26(7):745–749,797

Martin FM, Sánchez JM, Wilkinson O (2023) The economic impact of COVID-19 around the world. Federal Reserve Bank of St. Louis Review, Second Quarter, pp 74–88

Chapter 7
Practice of Risk Management on Mpox

Mpox is a zoonotic infectious disease caused by the mpox virus, predominantly endemic in African countries such as Nigeria, the Democratic Republic of the Congo (DR Congo), and the Central African Republic (WHO 2019). The mpox virus, as the Orthopoxvirus genus within the Poxviridae family, possesses a linear double-stranded DNA genome approximately 197 kb in size (Alakunle et al. 2020). The virus is classified into two clades: the Central African clade (formerly known as the Congo Basin clade and now redesignated as Clade I) and the West African clade (Clade II) (WHO 2019; Bunge et al. 2022; WHO n.d.). Clade I, which is associated with higher fatality and severe disease rates, is predominantly found in countries such as the Republic of the Congo, Gabon, and the Central African Republic (WHO 2019; Bunge et al. 2022; WHO n.d.). On June 25, 2022, the World Health Organization (WHO) convened an emergency meeting and determined that the multi-country mpox cases did not constitute a Public Health Emergency of International Concern (PHEIC). However, on July 23, 2022, in light of the global spread and characteristics of mpox cases, WHO declared the mpox outbreak as a PHEIC. This designation was later lifted on May 11, 2023, yet the WHO emphasized the continued need for prevention and control measures akin to those for HIV/AIDS and other sexually transmitted diseases (Meeting of the International Health Regulations 2005; Second meeting of the International Health Regulations 2005). Despite an overall downward trend in the global mpox outbreak as of March 12, 2024, the mpox first pandemic spread on a global scale also underscores the challenges posed by the development of socio-economic conditions on the risk assessment, surveillance, and early warning of infectious disease epidemics. This chapter of the book provides a reference for the prevention and management of mpox by delineating the disease's distribution and burden, summarizing its risk assessment, surveillance and early warning, as well as the evaluation of control strategies and their effectiveness.

J. Liu, *Risk Management in Public Health*, Innovation in Risk Analysis,
https://doi.org/10.1007/978-981-97-6826-4_7

7.1 Disease Durden

Since the first confirmed human case of mpox was reported in the DR Congo in 1970, subsequent cases have been documented in Nigeria, the Central African Republic, and the Republic of the Congo in 1971, 1984, and 2003, respectively (Ladnyj et al. 1972; Durski et al. 2018). Then, mpox have predominantly occurred in Central and West African countries, while other countries such as the United States (US), Singapore, and the United Kingdom (UK) have primarily experienced imported cases (Gross 2003; Ng et al. 2019; Vaughan et al. 2018; Erez et al. 2019). Since the report of a mpox case in the UK in May 2022, as of February 7, 2024, a total of 93,497 confirmed mpox cases have been reported across 118 countries or terriotories, encompassing Africa, Europe, America, the Western Pacific, and the Eastern Mediterranean (USACDC 2022a). Genomic sequencing results indicate that the mpox cases in multiple countries in 2022 belong to Clade II and are closely related to the strains exported from Nigeria to the UK, Israel, and Singapore in 2018 and 2019 (Isidro et al. 2022).

7.1.1 Characteristics of Population

7.1.1.1 Gender and Age

Previous research has indicated that before 2022, the age range of mpox cases was broad, predominantly affecting adolescents or young adult males (Osadebe et al. 2017; Jezek et al. 1987; Whitehouse et al. 2021; Yinka-Ogunleye et al. 2019). However, in 2022, the median age of mpox cases in multiple countries was between 35 and 41 years, primarily involving middle-aged males (Girometti et al. 2022; Patel et al. 2022; Philpott et al. 2022; Thornhill et al. 2022). WHO reported that as of October 6, 2023, the proportion of male cases in the mpox outbreak was 96.4% (84,316/87,465), with a median age (Q1, Q3) of 34 years (29 to 41 years), and 79.4% of all cases were males aged 18 to 44 (WHO 2022a). A meta-analysis conducted in 2019 showed that from 1970 to 2019, the median age of mpox cases increased from 4 years (1970–2010) to 21 years (2010–2019), further suggesting a shift towards an older demographic profile in affected populations (Bunge et al. 2022). Despite the global outbreak predominantly affecting middle-aged males, in the African region, the number of female cases is nearly equivalent to that of males, with cases still concentrated among adolescents. As of January 31, 2024, the African region reported 359 male cases and 313 female cases. Among those with known ages, the median age (Q1, Q3) was 17 years (7 to 32 years), with 50.4% of cases being under 18 years old and 17.7% being under 5 years old (Bunge et al. 2022).

7.1.1.2 Animal Contact History, Travel History, and Man Who Make Sex with Man

Prior to 2022, mpox cases were predominantly reported in countries in the Central and West African regions, where the likelihood of human contact with forest wildlife is high, leading to a majority of cases having a history of animal contact (Whitehouse et al. 2021; Yinka-Ogunleye et al. 2019; Doshi et al. 2020). Sporadic travel-related imported cases have been reported in countries outside Africa. However, the proportion of international travel history among the 2022 multi-country mpox cases was not substantial, ranging from approximately 20% to 46% (Girometti et al. 2022; Patel et al. 2022; Philpott et al. 2022; Thornhill et al. 2022). The risk history for the 2022 multi-country mpox cases was primarily characterized by sexual behavior among men who make sex with men (MSM) (Girometti et al. 2022; Patel et al. 2022; Thornhill et al. 2022; Perez Duque et al. 2022; Minhaj et al. 2022; Mahase 2022; Ferraro et al. 2022). The WHO reported that, as of October 6, 2023, sexual transmission accounted for up to 83% (18,230/21,891) of the mpox cases in the 2022 outbreak (WHO 2022a). Among individuals with known sexual behavior, 85.4% (29,181/34,174) had a history of sexual behavior among men who make sex with men (MSM), suggesting that MSM may constitute a high-risk population for this particular epidemic (WHO 2022a).

7.1.2 Characteristics of Spatial Distribution

Prior to 2022, the majority of mpox cases were reported in Central and West African countries. In 2003, outside the African region, the US reported 47 confirmed and probable mpox cases, all of which were closely associated with the importation of various rodent species from Ghana (Gross 2003; USACDC 2022b). Additionally, the UK and Israel reported imported mpox cases related to travel history in Nigeria in 2018, and Singapore did so in 2019 (Ng et al. 2019; Vaughan et al. 2018; Erez et al. 2019).

From January 1, 2022, to January 31, 2024, a total of 93,921 laboratory-confirmed cases and 662 probable cases, including 179 deaths, were reported to the WHO by 117 countries or regions (WHO 2022a). According to the latest reporting dates by region, region of the Americas, Europe, Africa, the Western Pacific, Southeast Asia, and the Eastern Mediterranean have reported 60,887, 26,843, 2834, 2429, 833, and 95 confirmed mpox cases, respectively (WHO 2022a). As of January 31, 2024, the total number of confirmed cases in the top 10 countries with mpox cases accounted for 81% of all reported cases globally. The top 10 countries are the US (n = 31,576), Brazil (n = 10,967), Spain (n = 7786), France (n = 4179), Colombia (n = 4090), Mexico (n = 4079), the United Kingdom (n = 3882), Peru (n = 3812), Germany (n = 3807), and China (n = 2028) (WHO 2022a).

7.1.3 Characteristics of Time Trends

Surveillance data for suspected mpox cases in the DR, Congo indicate that from 2001 to 2013, a total of 19,646 suspected cases were reported. The incidence increased significantly from 0.64 (95% CI: 0.09–4.50) per 100,000 people in 2001 to 2.82 (95% CI: 0.40–20.10) per 100,000 people in 2013, demonstrating an upward trend (Hoff et al. 2017). Whitehouse et al. (2021) reported on 1057 confirmed mpox cases in the Tshuapa province of the DRC between 2011 and 2015, with an annual average incidence rate of 14.1 (95% CI: 13.3–15.0) per 100,000 people, which is 2.73 (95% CI: 2.21–3.40) times higher than the rate observed from 1980 to 1985.

The WHO latest report on the global trend of mpox cases in the 2022–2023 multi-country outbreak, shows as of January 31, 2024, a pattern of increase followed by a decline in global mpox cases when plotted against the dates of symptom onset, laboratory or clinical diagnosis, and reporting (Fig. 7.1) (WHO 2022a).

As of January 31, 2024, the peak monthly report of mpox cases occurred in August 2022, with a total of 30,910 cases reported (WHO 2022a). In the recent six-month period, from August 1, 2023, to January 31, 2024, the average number of new cases reported per month was 791, with the Western Pacific Region (n = 1418), the Region of the Americas (n = 1241), and the European Region (n = 871) reporting the highest number of new cases (WHO 2022a). Additionally, there may be an emerging upward trend in the number of cases reported recently in the Region of the Americas and the European Region (Fig. 7.2) (WHO 2022a).

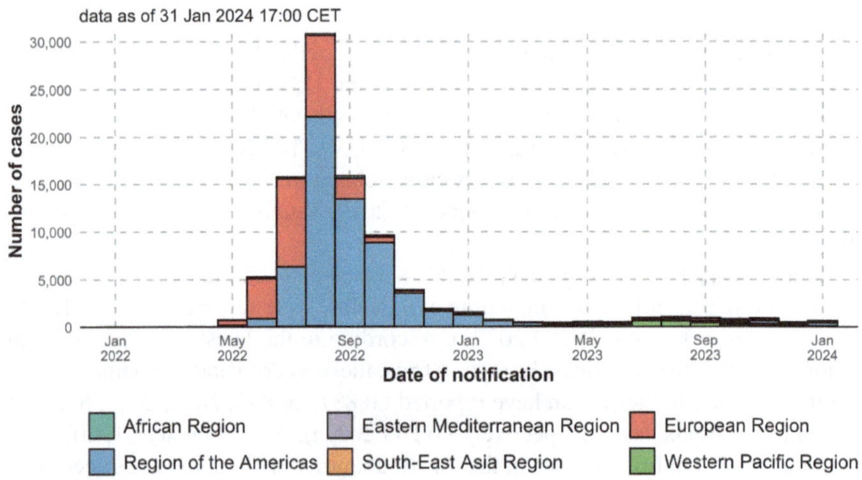

Fig. 7.1 Trends in the global mpox epidemic

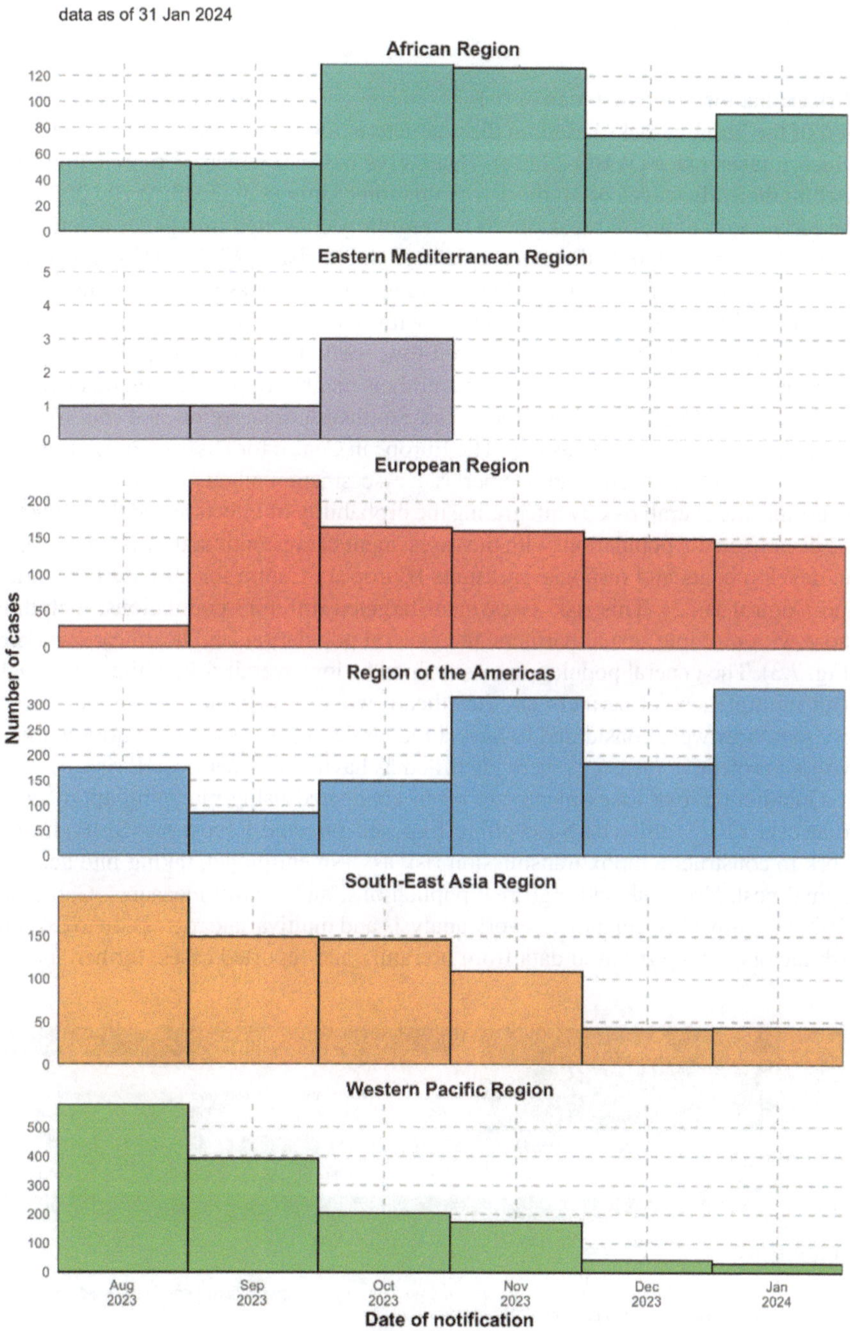

Fig. 7.2 Global trends in mpox cases by WHO regions

7.2 Risk Assessment

Risk evaluation is the first-step of risk-based approach: identification and quantification of the baseline risks based on the characteristics of the event and the context in which it takes place (WHO 2022b). Qualitative risk assessment is more commonly used in the early stages of mpox risk evaluation (Amer et al. 2023; WHO 2023). In the early stages of the outbreak, the WHO regularly convened emergency meetings to assess the current state of the mpox epidemic and its risks (WHO 2022a). As of July 2023, the global risk of mpox in MSM and sex workers was assessed as moderate. The general population risk in countries with newly reported or unreported mpox cases during 2022–2023 was considered low, while the general population risk in countries with previous mpox reports and their neighboring countries was deemed moderate (WHO 2022a). The risk in the Southeast Asia region and the Western Pacific region was assessed as low. The European Centre for Disease Prevention and Control (ECDC) utilized a rapid expert risk assessment method on May 22, 2022, to determine the overall risk by integrating the probability of infection and the impact of the disease on the population, with the assessment being continuously updated based on developments and response measures (European Centre for Disease Prevention and Control 2022). This risk assessment targeted different populations, including those with multiple sexual partners, the general population, and healthcare workers (Fig. 7.3). The general population was assigned a low overall risk, while individuals with multiple sexual partners and healthcare workers without appropriate protective measures were considered to have a moderate overall risk. Laboratory workers without protective measures were identified as having a higher overall risk.

Quantitative risk assessments are often conducted using modeling approaches. Yuan et al. (2023) utilized a Susceptible-Exposed-Infected-Recovered (SEIR) framework to construct a mpox transmission risk assessment model, taking into account animal hosts, low-risk and high-risk populations, and control measures. Gao et al. (2023) employed correlation network analysis and multivariate regression to explore risk factors for mpox based data from literature and reported cases, further applied

	Persons with multiple sexual partners, including some MSM	Broader population	Health professionals			
			HCWs		Laboratory personnel	
			Proper PPE	Unprotected exposure	Proper procedure and PPE	Unprotected exposure
Probability	High	Very low	Very low	High	Very low	High
Impact	Low	Low	Low	Low	Low	Moderate
Overall risk	Moderate	Low	Low	Moderate	Low	High

The risk may be higher for certain people in some of the above categories, particularly very young children, pregnant women, elderly, or immunocompromised persons.

Fig. 7.3 Early European Centers for Disease Control and Prevention mpox risk assessment in different populations (HCWs: high commitment work systems; PPE: personal protective equipment)

an improved SEIR model and risk factor-driven k-means clustering analysis for the risk assessment of mpox in various countries (Gao et al. 2023). Some researchers have evaluated the importation risk of mypox in the early stages. For example, in the early stages of 2022, Du et al. (2022) used a risk matrix and the Borda count method to assess the importation risk of mpox based on global mpox cases, deaths, and the number of international students coming to China. In 2023, Huang et al. (2023) established a real-time risk assessment model using flight data, mpox epidemic data, and national control measures to evaluate the importation risk of mpox in China. Individual risk assessments are less common. Zucker et al. (2023) utilized cohort data to establish a Cox regression model to explore risk factors for mpox infection, thereby facilitating individual risk assessment efforts (Zucker et al. 2023).

7.3 Surveillance and Early Warning

In the early stages of the mpox epidemic, African countries were predominantly affected. During the 2022–2023 mpox outbreak, the majority of reporting countries were developing countries with limited capacity for surveillance and reporting of mpox cases. The sparsity, widespread distribution, and unpredictability of cases hindered accurate risk–benefit calculations for mpox. Furthermore, mpox was not included in the list of notifiable infectious diseases in most countries, which may have led to the persistent neglect of the disease. However, the lack of robust surveillance and awareness may increase the transmission of mpox. Typical symptoms of mpox cases include fever, skin rash, and lymphadenopathy, making symptom-based surveillance crucial for early warning. Cases are detected through temperature monitoring, medical patrols, and voluntary reporting, with the monitoring of abnormal fluctuations in case numbers serving as an early signal of epidemic changes (Hu et al. 2023). The main objectives of surveillance are to promptly identify cases and clusters of infection, as well as the source of infection, in order to provide optimal clinical care; to isolate cases to prevent further transmission and establish; to manage and track contacts to identify early signs of infection and determine groups at risk of infection and severe disease; and to protect frontline health workers and develop effective control measures. The WHO report——*Surveillance, case investigation and contact tracing for mpox (monkeypox): interim guidance* mentioned indicators for assessing the quality of surveillance, including: (1) The proportion of probable cases aand confirmed cases with complete demographic information; (2) The proportion of suspected cases that have undergone laboratory testing; (3) The proportion of probable and confirmed cases with complete clinical and risk factor information (WHEP 2022). Additionally, in the context of a global epidemic, it is important to strengthen international cooperation and social surveillance in the work of monitoring and early warning (WHEP 2022).

7.3.1 Strengthen International Cooperation and Monitoring

On October 5, 2022, the WHO released the *Monkeypox Strategic Preparedness, Readiness, and Response Plan (SPRP)* to address the global mpox outbreak and enhance global collaborative surveillance ability (WHO 2022c). This plan encouraged national surveillance, epidemiological investigations, and contact tracing; advocated for the genomic sequencing of the mpox virus identified in the current outbreak and expanded testing across all six WHO regions; encouraged provision of diagnostic capabilities and training. Ultimately, by strengthening international collaboration in risk prediction and disease surveillance, the plan aimed to understand factors that may contribute to the spread of the mpox virus, such as the number of sexual partners, various types of activities and gatherings, and animal contact. The ECDC also consolidates and shares information reported by member states on a weekly basis. Yu Xin et al. (2022) proposed the construction of a systematic, scientific, comprehensive, and efficient epidemic monitoring network through the General Administration of Customs' Smart Health Inspection System. This involves collecting epidemic information from countries and regions with air connections, closely monitoring the progress of mpox transmission across countries and continents, vigilantly following changes in overseas mpox epidemics, and actively conducting risk assessments for mpox at ports of entry. This study suggested making full use of application technologies such as big data, cloud computing, and the "Internet Plus" to analyze the characteristics and trends of mpox virus transmission and epidemic changes, enhance the analysis and early warning of risk factors for mpox at ports of entry, scientifically evaluate the risk levels of mpox importion and subsequent transmission at ports, strictly monitor and promptly issue early warning signals, guide precise quarantine at ports, dynamically adjust prevention and control measures, and ensure early detection, early warning, and early disposal of mpox outbreaks (Xin et al. 2022).

7.3.2 Regular Social Surveillance

The SPRP proposed that regular social surveillance should be integrated into a multi-source surveillance system (WHO 2022c). Online and community surveys are instrumental in the identification and detection of suspected mpox cases and the effective control of community outbreaks. It is crucial for all countries responding to mpox outbreak in rapidly detection, investigation and assessment of signals from social surveillance (WHO 2022c). Previous studies have analyzed the relationship between Baidu Index (Jietao et al. 2023), Google Index (Yan et al. 2023), and mpox cases. Zheng Jietao et al. (2023) found a nonlinear correlation ($R^2 = 0.122$, $P = 0.001$) between the cumulative number of global mpox cases and the national Baidu search index, with negative correlation when the number of cases was low or high, and positive correlation when the number was moderate. Yan et al. (2023) discovered a correlation between Google Index and the number of reported mpox cases, with the highest correlation when the lag days were 13 days, which might be the optimal period for early warning and surveillance of mpox outbreaks.

7.4 Prevention and Control Strategy and Measures

During the early stages of the global mpox outbreak, the WHO stated that control and prevention measures should be enhanced in the following three areas: (1) interrupting human-to-human transmission, with a priority focus on communities at high risk of contact; (2) protecting vulnerable populations at risk; and (3) minimizing transmission between humans and animals (WHO 2022c). In response to the clinical management and prevention of mpox cases, the WHO has proposed three recommendations for case screening, isolation, and clinical assessment: (1) primary health systems should screen and triage all individuals presenting with a rash, fever, or lymphadenopathy according to the case definition to identify suspected or confirmed cases; (2) after screening and isolation, suspected cases should be triaged using standardized triage tools, and further assessed for risk factors and the presence of severe illness; and (3) laboratory confirmation should be conducted for suspected cases (WHO 2022d). Additionally, the WHO has outlined management measures for mild mpox cases, issues related to the skin lesions and mental health of patients, and preventive efforts for special populations, such as healthcare workers, pregnant women, and young children (WHO 2022d). The WHO has emphasized that while mpox was predominantly found among MSM in 2022, the general population should be aware of the reporting and characteristics of mpox in their area, maintain good hygiene practices, and avoid close contact with individuals suspected of or confirmed to have mpox (WHO 2022e). If there is a suspicion of mpox virus infection, individuals should self-isolate, avoid close contact with others, and then seek medical assistance (WHO 2022e).

The WHO had suggested that although the smallpox vaccine is effective in preventing mpox, there is currently no need for, nor is there a recommendation to conduct mass vaccinations (WHO 2019, 2022f). For individuals who have been in contact with cases, post-exposure prophylactic vaccination with appropriate second- or third-generation vaccines is recommended (within four days of initial exposure) (WHO 2019, 2022f). Primary pre-exposure vaccination is advised for those at high risk of exposure, including but not limited to MSM, individuals with multiple sexual partners, high-risk healthcare workers, laboratory personnel working with orthopoxviruses, clinical laboratory professionals conducting diagnostic testing for mpox, and others who may be at risk (WHO 2019, 2022f). As of April 2023, preclinical research on global mpox vaccines has been primarily conducted in the US and China. The technical approaches for mpox candidate vaccines in preclinical studies include attenuated live vaccines, subunit vaccines, viral vector vaccines, and nucleic acid vaccines (DNA and mRNA vaccines). Preclinical studies on various mpox vaccines have indicated that different types of mpox candidate vaccines can provide effective immune protection for test animals against mpox or vaccinia viruses, laying a solid foundation for subsequent clinical research on mpox vaccines. Currently, some research institutions in China have begun the development of mpox vaccines, mainly focusing on the development of mpox mRNA vaccines. As of April 2023, a total of 14 clinical studies on mpox vaccines have been initiated globally. To date, two types of vaccines that have undergone clinical trials for the prevention of mpox are available: the Modified Vaccinia Ankara-Bavarian Nordic (MVA-BN, marketed as JYNNEOS), produced by Bavarian Nordic, Denmark, and the fourth-generation smallpox vaccine produced in Japan. JYNNEOS is a vaccine approved by the U.S. Food and Drug Administration for the prevention of mpox (Mingting and Fuqiang 2023; Shiyun et al. 2022). On 11 November 2022, the vaccine was licensed in the Russian Federation as OrthopoxVac, for immunization against smallpox, mpox, and other orthopoxviruses (WHO 2023b). From May 19 to 31, 2023, an online survey conducted by the WHO on MSM, bisexuals, and other men who engage in sexual activity with men, transgender and gender diverse individuals in the Americas and Europe revealed that among 16,985 respondents, only 29.6% had received at least one dose of the vaccine, and 20.8% had received two doses (WHO 2023a). There are significant challenges in accessing vaccines in Latin America and Eastern Europe (WHO 2023a).

7.5 Effect Evaluation

To date, there has been no specific study dedicated to the evaluation of the effectiveness of mpox control and management. Based on the general principles of effectiveness evaluation and the announcement by the WHO on May 11, 2023, that the mpox outbreak no longer constitutes a PHEIC, the decline in the number of cases following the implementation of control measures by countries, with the transmission characteristics and high-risk populations identified, suggests that the global control of mpox has achieved relatively good outcomes. Majee et al. (2023) utilized the SEIR model, incorporating vaccination and parameters of population control measures, and compared the effectiveness of vaccination, intensified treatment, and a combination of both measures by calculating the Infected Averted Ratio (IAR) and the Incremental Cost-Effectiveness Ratio (ICER). The study found that the IAR and ICER for intensified treatment were both greater than those for vaccination and combined measures (Majee et al. 2023). It is important to note that the decline in the number of mpox cases and the proportion of severe cases is only one aspect of effectiveness evaluation. From individual perspective, the long-term health impacts following a mpox infection should also be considered in the future. Additionally, the effectiveness of mpox control and management can also be reflected in the reduction of related risky behaviors and the sustained rate of safe sexual practices (WHO 2023a).

In the context of monkeypox control and management, the evaluation of the effectiveness of vaccination has been a focal point. Van et al. (2023) reported that the effectiveness of the first-generation smallpox vaccine in preventing moderate to severe mpox infections was 58% (95% CI: 17–78%). Wolff et al. (2023) reported that the estimated effectiveness of a single subcutaneous dose of the JYNNEOS vaccine, after adjusting for confounding factors, was 86% (95% CI: 59–95%) at ninety days among males. Xu et al. (2023) reported that the effectiveness of a single dose of the JYNNEOS vaccine was 87% (95% CI: 84–90%), and the effectiveness of two doses was 89% (95% CI: 78–100%) in a meta-analysis. Furthermore, Rosenberg et al. (2023) reported that the combined adjusted effectiveness of one ($\geq$14 days prior) or two doses of the JYNNEOS vaccine was 75.7% (95% CI: 48.5–88.5%), with one dose being 68.1% (95% CI: 24.9–86.5%) and two doses being 88.5% (95% CI: 44.1–97.6%) among males. Deputy et al. (2023) reported that the adjusted vaccine effectiveness for two doses of JYNNEOS was 66.0% (95% CI: 47.4–78.1%), and for one dose, it was 35.8% (95% CI: 22.1–47.1%).

Overall, the global mpox epidemic since 2022 quickly garnered the attention of countries. The epidemic waned in the half yaer of 2023. The identification of mpox transmission characteristics, coupled with the control experience accumulated from COVID-19, seemed to help countries to face mpox. The control of the mpox epidemic has demonstrated the entire process of an infectious disease in 21th century, from surveillance and early warning to risk assessment, control of importion and local outbreaks, and achieving control effectiveness.

References

Alakunle E, Moens U, Nchinda G, Okeke MI (2020) Monkeypox virus in nigeria: infection biology, epidemiology, and evolution. Viruses 12(11)

Amer F, Khalil HES, Elahmady M et al (2023) Mpox: risks and approaches to prevention. J Infect Public Health 16(6):901–910

Bunge EM, Hoet B, Chen L, et al. (2022) The changing epidemiology of human monkeypox—a potential threat? A systematic review. PLoS Negl Trop Dis 16(2)

Deputy NP, Deckert J, Chard AN et al (2023) Vaccine effectiveness of JYNNEOS against Mpox disease in the United States. N Engl J Med 388(26):2434–2443

Doshi RH, Alfonso VH, Morier D et al (2020) Monkeypox rash severity and animal exposures in the Democratic Republic of the Congo. EcoHealth 17(1):64–73

Du M, Zhang SM, Shang WJ et al (2022) Multiple-country Monkeypox outbreak and its importation risk into China: an assessment based on the risk matrix method. Biomed Environ Sci (BES) 35(10):878–887

Durski KN, McCollum AM, Nakazawa Y et al (2018) Emergence of Monkeypox - West and Central Africa, 1970–2017. MMWR Morb Mortal Wkly Rep 67(10):306–310

Erez N, Achdout H, Milrot E, et al. (2019) Diagnosis of imported Monkeypox, Israel, 2018. Emerg Infect Dis 25(5):980–983

European Centre for Disease Prevention and Control (2022, May 23) Risk assessment: Monkeypox multi-country outbreak. https://www.ecdc.europa.eu/sites/default/files/documents/Monkeypox-multi-country-outbreak.pdf

Ferraro F, Caraglia A, Rapiti A, et al. (2022) Letter to the editor: multiple introductions of MPX in Italy from different geographic areas. Euro surveillance: bulletin Europeen sur les maladies transmissibles. Eur Commun Dis Bull 27(23)

Gao J, Zhou C, Liang H et al (2023) Monkeypox outbreaks in the context of the COVID-19 pandemic: network and clustering analyses of global risks and modified SEIR prediction of epidemic trends. Front Public Health 11:1052946

Girometti N, Byrne R, Bracchi M et al (2022) Demographic and clinical characteristics of confirmed human monkeypox virus cases in individuals attending a sexual health centre in London, UK: an observational analysis. Lancet Infect Dis 22(9):1321–1329

Gross E (2003) Update: multistate outbreak of monkeypox–Illinois, Indiana, Kansas, Missouri, Ohio, and Wisconsin, 2003. MMWR Morb Mortal Wkly Rep 52(27):642–646

Hoff NA, Doshi RH, Colwell B, et al. (2017) Evolution of a disease surveillance system: an increase in reporting of human Monkeypox disease in the Democratic Republic of the Congo, 2001–2013. Int J Trop Dis & Health 25(2)

Hu XF, Qiu WY, Luo Y et al (2023) Epidemiological analysis of the global monkeypox epidemic and imported cases in China. Chin J Front Health Quar 46(2):122–126

Huang Q, Sun Y, Jia M et al (2023) Risk assessment for cross-border transmission of multi-country Mpox outbreaks in 2022. J Infect Public Health 16(4):618–625

Isidro J, Borges V, Pinto M et al (2022) Phylogenomic characterization and signs of microevolution in the 2022 multi-country outbreak of monkeypox virus. Nat Med 28(8):1569–1572

Jezek Z, Szczeniowski M, Paluku KM, Mutombo M (1987) Human monkeypox: clinical features of 282 patients. J Infect Dis 156(2):293–298

Jietao Z, Yifan Y, Li L (2023) Research on global monkeypox epidemic network public opinion in 2022 based on Baidu index. Mod Med Hyg 39(10):1626–1629

Ladnyj ID, Ziegler P, Kima E (1972) A human infection caused by monkeypox virus in Basankusu Territory, Democratic Republic of the Congo. Bull World Health Organ 46(5):593–597

Mahase E (2022) Seven monkeypox cases are confirmed in England. BMJ (clinical Research Ed) 377:o1239

Majee S, Jana S, Kar TK (2023) Dynamical analysis of monkeypox transmission incorporating optimal vaccination and treatment with cost-effectiveness. Chaos (Woodbury, NY) 33(4)

Meeting of the International Health Regulations (2005) Emergency Committee regarding the multi-country monkeypox outbreak (accessed 25 June 2022 Statement Reading time: 7 min (1895 words)

Mingting W, Fuqiang C (2023) Epidemiological characteristics and prevention and control status of monkeypox. Jiangsu Prev Med 34(1):8–11

Minhaj FS, Ogale YP, Whitehill F, et al. (2022) Monkeypox Outbreak - Nine States, May 2022. MMWR Morb Mortal Wkly Rep 71(23):764–769

Ng OT, Lee V, Marimuthu K et al (2019) A case of imported Monkeypox in Singapore. Lancet Infect Dis 19(11):1166

Osadebe L, Hughes CM, Shongo Lushima R et al (2017) Enhancing case definitions for surveillance of human monkeypox in the Democratic Republic of Congo. PLoS Negl Trop Dis 11(9):e0005857

Patel A, Bilinska J, Tam JCH, et al. (2022) Clinical features and novel presentations of human monkeypox in a central London centre during the 2022 outbreak: descriptive case series. BMJ (Clinical research ed): e072410

Perez Duque M, Ribeiro S, Martins JV, et al. (2022) Ongoing monkeypox virus outbreak, Portugal, 29 April to 23 May 2022. Euro surveillance: bulletin Europeen sur les maladies transmissibles. Eur Commun Dis Bull 27(22)

Philpott D, Hughes CM, Alroy KA, et al. (2022) Epidemiologic and clinical characteristics of Monkeypox cases - United States, May 17-July 22, 2022. MMWR Morb Mortal Wkly Rep 71(32):1018–1022

Rosenberg ES, Dorabawila V, Hart-Malloy R, et al. (2023) Effectiveness of JYNNEOS vaccine against diagnosed Mpox infection - New York, 2022. MMWR Morb Mortal Wkly Rep 72(20):559–563

Second meeting of the International Health Regulations (IHR) (2005) Emergency Committee regarding the multi-country outbreak of monkeypox. https://www.who.int/news/item/23-07-2022-second-meeting-of-the-international-health-regulations-(2005)-(ihr)-emergency-committee-regarding-the-multi-country-outbreak-of-monkeypox (accessed 2 September 2022)

Shiyun L, Jia LU, Xinguo LI, Xiaoming Y (2022) Research progress of monkeypox virus and its vaccine. Chin J Biol 35(12):1409–1413

Thornhill JP, Barkati S, Walmsley S et al (2022) Monkeypox virus infection in humans across 16 countries - April-June 2022. N Engl J Med 387(8):679–691

USACDC (2022a) Monkeypox and Orthopoxvirus outbreak global map. https://www.cdc.gov/poxvirus/monkeypox/response/2022/world-map.html

USACDC (2022b) Past U.S. Cases and Outbreaks. https://www.cdc.gov/poxvirus/monkeypox/outbreak/us-outbreaks.html (accessed 16 June 2022)

van Ewijk CE, Miura F, van Rijckevorsel G, et al. (2023) Mpox outbreak in the Netherlands, 2022: public health response, characteristics of the first 1000 cases and protection of the first-generation smallpox vaccine. Euro surveillance: bulletin Europeen sur les maladies transmissibles. Eur Commun Dis Bull 28(12)

Vaughan A, Aarons E, Astbury J, et al. (2018) Two cases of monkeypox imported to the United Kingdom, September 2018. Euro surveillance : bulletin Europeen sur les maladies transmissibles. Eur Commun Dis Bull 23(38)

WHEP (2022, December) Surveillance, case investigation and contact tracing for mpox (monkeypox): interim guidance. https://www.who.int/publications/i/item/WHO-MPX-Surveillance-2022.422

Whitehouse ER, Bonwitt J, Hughes CM et al (2021) Clinical and epidemiological findings from enhanced Monkeypox surveillance in Tshuapa Province, Democratic Republic of the Congo During 2011–2015. J Infect Dis 223(11):1870–1878

WHO. (n.d.) Monkeypox: experts give virus variants new names. https://www.who.int/news/item/12-08-2022-monkeypox--experts-give-virus-variants-new-names (accessed 2 September 2022).

WHO (2019) Monkeypox 2019 [updated December 9, 2019]. https://www.who.int/news-room/fact-sheets/detail/monkeypox

WHO (2022a) 2022 Monkeypox outbreak: global trends. https://worldhealthorg.shinyapps.io/mpx_global/ (accessed 31 August 2022)

WHO (2022b) Public health advice for gatherings during the current monkeypox outbreak.

WHO (2022c) Monkeypox strategic preparedness, readiness, and response plan (SPRP)

WHO (2022d, June 10) Clinical management and infection prevention and control for monkeypox: Interim rapid response guidance. https://www.who.int/publications/i/item/WHO-MPX-Clinical-and-IPC-2022.1 (accessed 23 August 2022)

WHO (2022e) Public health advice for gay, bisexual and other men who have sex with men on the recent outbreak of monkeypox. https://cdn.who.int/media/docs/default-source/hq-hiv-hepatitis-and-stis-library/flyer_msm_a4_eng-v5.pdf?sfvrsn=7648499_32&download=true (accessed 22 August 2022)

WHO (2022f, August 24) Vaccines and immunization for monkeypox: interim guidance (accessed 31 August 2022)

WHO (2023a) Community experiences of the 2022–2023 mpox outbreak in Europe and the Americas: technical brief. Geneva: World Health Organization. Licence: CC BY-NC-SA 3.0 IGO

WHO (2023b) WHO Advisory Committee on Variola Virus Research: report of the twenty-fourth meeting, Geneva, 29–30 November 2022. Geneva: World Health Organization. Licence: CC BY-NC-SA 3.0 IGO

Wolff Sagy Y, Zucker R, Hammerman A et al (2023) Real-world effectiveness of a single dose of mpox vaccine in males. Nat Med 29(3):748–752

Xin Y, Yongli J, Zhongqi L, Li Z, Mingqiang Z (2022) Epidemic status of monkeypox virus and prevention and control strategies at ports in China. Port Health Control 27(4):14–17

Xu M, Liu C, Du Z, Bai Y, Wang Z, Gao C. (2023) Real-world effectiveness of mpox (monkeypox) vaccines: a systematic review. J Travel Med 30(5):taad048

Yan W, Du M, Qin C et al (2023) Association between public attention and monkeypox epidemic: a global lag-correlation analysis. J Med Virol 95(1):e28382

Yinka-Ogunleye A, Aruna O, Dalhat M et al (2019) Outbreak of human monkeypox in Nigeria in 2017–18: a clinical and epidemiological report. Lancet Infect Dis 19(8):872–879

Yuan P, Tan Y, Yang L et al (2023) Assessing transmission risks and control strategy for monkeypox as an emerging zoonosis in a metropolitan area. J Med Virol 95(1):e28137

Zucker R, Lavie G, Wolff-Sagy Y et al (2023) Risk assessment of human mpox infections: retrospective cohort study. Clin Microbiol Infect 29(8):1070–1074

Chapter 8
Practice of Risk Management on Malaria

Malaria is a severe disease caused by parasites, mainly transmitted by certain species of female mosquitoes. These mosquitoes carry the malaria parasites, which are transmitted to the human body during the mosquitoes' blood feeding, causing malaria. The disease is widespread worldwide, especially in tropical regions, posing a significant threat to life. Malaria is caused by five different types of *Plasmodium*, among which *Plasmodium falciparum* and *Plasmodium vivax* are the most common and dangerous. Malaria caused by Plasmodium falciparum is the most severe, with a high mortality rate, while Plasmodium vivax causes a prolonged and recurrent course of malaria (World Health Organization n.d.a).

The harm of malaria lies not only in its threat to human health but also in its challenge to socioeconomics. Therefore, effective malaria control and management strategies are vital issues in global public health. In response to this challenge, the World Health Organization issued *Global technical strategy for malaria 2016–2030* in 2015 (World Health Organization n.d.b). The strategy clarifies the specific goal of reducing the global incidence and mortality rates of malaria by at least 90% by 2030 and proposes corresponding strategies and actions. The strategy also emphasizes the principles of local adaptation and full participation in malaria prevention and control. This chapter will primarily focus on the prevention and management of malaria, delve into the global malaria burden, risk assessment, monitoring and early warning, prevention and control measures, and impact evaluation, etc., to assist malaria control and management workers worldwide to effectively tackle this global public health problem.

J. Liu, *Risk Management in Public Health*, Innovation in Risk Analysis,
https://doi.org/10.1007/978-981-97-6826-4_8

8.1 Disease Burden

The estimated global number of malaria cases in 2022 reached 249 million, an increase of 5 million from 2021. This upward trend aligns with the recent rise in cases, especially in the WHO African region, which accounted for 93.6% and 95.4% of global malaria cases and deaths respectively in 2022. Conversely, global malaria deaths decreased from 2000 to 2019, but due to the COVID-19 pandemic, it rose to 631,000 in 2020, and despite a decline in 2021 and 2022, it still remains above the 2019 level (World Health Organization n.d.a).

The burden of malaria in the WHO African region is profound. Countries such as Nigeria, the Democratic Republic of Congo, Uganda, and Mozambique bear a particularly severe malaria burden, contributing the majority of global cases and deaths. For instance, Nigeria accounted for 26.8% of global malaria cases, and the Democratic Republic of Congo accounted for 11.6% of deaths. Additionally, Nigeria also accounted for a staggering 38.5% of worldwide malaria deaths in children below five years old (Liu et al. 2021).

Data from other regions show a decrease in malaria cases and deaths in the Southeast Asia region, with Sri Lanka being certified as malaria-free in 2016, indicating significant progress in malaria control. Meanwhile, the Eastern Mediterranean region saw an increase in malaria cases from 2015 to 2022, mainly due to malaria outbreaks triggered by floods in Pakistan. The Western Pacific also saw a decline, with China being verified malaria-free in 2021. The Americas have seen a significant reduction in malaria cases and deaths, partly attributed to COVID-19 pandemic restrictions which limited populations' movement and increased availability of malaria diagnostics and treatment supplies (Liu and Liu 2023).

Challenges faced globally in responding to malaria include financing shortfalls, drug and insecticide resistance, and disruptions to malaria service due to the COVID-19 pandemic. Insufficient funding limits preventative and curative measures, resistance threatens malaria control and the impacts of the pandemic exacerbate the burden of the disease. To effectively address these challenges, the report suggests enhancing international cooperation, boosting funding, improving malaria prevention and treatment services, and tackling resistance. Meanwhile, there's also a need to acknowledge the impacts of the COVID-19 pandemic on malaria services and take measures to minimize these impacts, ensuring the continuity and effectiveness of global malaria control and elimination efforts.

8.2 Risk Assessment

At present, due to the substantial differences in malaria prevalence in different countries, risk assessment is mainly divided into malaria importation risk assessment for areas with low malaria prevalence or areas where malaria has been eliminated, and intra-transmission risk assessment for areas with high malaria prevalence. The methods for assessing the risk of malaria importation and transmission can primarily be divided into three categories: traditional risk assessment methods, biomathematical modeling methods, and Infectivity—Receptivity—Vulnerability (IRV) assessment methods (Chen et al. 2017).

8.2.1 *The Traditional Risk Assessment Method*

The traditional risk assessment method establishes a risk assessment system based on malaria epidemiological characteristics, determines indicators at various levels, and employs risk analysis methods to determine the weights and evaluate the indicator system. Most systems of malaria importation risk assessment indicator depend on the "three links" and "two factors" of the malaria transmission process to determine the required indicators, and then the weights of the indicators are determined based on the Delphi method, analytic hierarchy process (AHP) or entropy weight method.

The risk assessment based on the "three links" (i.e., the source of infection, mode of transmission, and susceptible population) is a commonly used method at present. It includes analyzing the distribution characteristics of local infectious cases, imported cases, and asymptomatic carriers, the ecological and behavioral characteristics of vectors, such as species, density, blood-feeding habits, susceptibility to malaria parasites and sensitivity to insecticides, as well as the behavior, malaria prevention knowledge and attitudes of susceptible populations, to assess the risk of malaria transmission. The assessment of malaria transmission risk based on the "two factors" (i.e., natural factors and social factors) is also very important. Natural and social factors influencing the transmission of malaria mainly include temperature, rainfall, relative humidity, topography and local economic level, etc. Since the transmission of malaria often results from the combined effects of the "three links" and the "two factors", these two aspects should be integrated organically when assessing the risk of malaria transmission.

8.2.2 *The Biomathematical Modeling Method*

In the biomathematical modeling method, models are further divided into individual stochastic models and population stochastic models depending on the unit of study. Individual stochastic models use multi-agent simulations for malaria retransmission risk assessment. These models consider both time and space dimensions, simulate the spatiotemporal characteristics of malaria transmission, and mimic the interactions between different individuals and media, combining "two factors" such as ecology, geography, population movement, to simulate the retransmission in different situations after malaria cases are imported. However, this model weakens important epidemiological parameters of malaria transmission such as the incubation period, infectious period, and relapse.

The population stochastic model is based on the epidemiological characteristics between the population and the media in the research area, as well as the characteristics of the two themselves. It simulates the probability of retransmission after malaria cases are imported into a certain area. However, its disadvantage is that it only considers the time dimension and lacks consideration of spatial transmission characteristics.

8.2.3 IRV Assessment Methods

The IRV method, developed in recent years, is mainly used to assess the risk of reintroduction of malaria in areas where it has been eliminated. It focuses on analyzing three aspects: the infectivity of vectors to imported malaria parasites, the receptivity of vectors, and the vulnerability. The IRV method was first proposed in 2001 and has been successively applied to the assessment of the risk of importation and reintroduction of malaria in malaria-eliminated European countries such as Italy, France, Greece, and Spain.

Infectivity refers to the sensitivity of vectors, mainly mosquitoes, to different malaria parasites. It is usually measured by the positivity rate of oocysts in the mosquito midgut and sporozoites in the mosquito salivary glands. Receptivity primarily combines and analyzes the influence of vector species, density, and biological characteristics on malaria transmission, usually measured by vectorial capacity. The calculation formula for vectorial capacity is: $-\frac{ma^2p^n}{\ln(p)}$, where ma is the biting rate (the number of times a person is bitten by a vector mosquito each night), m is the ratio of vector mosquitoes to the human population, a is the biting habit ($a = h/u$, h is the human blood index, u is the reproductive nutritional cycle of the vector), p is the daily survival rate in the mosquito population, and n is the time interval from the mosquito ingesting gametocytes to the appearance of sporozoites in the mosquito's salivary glands, $-\frac{1}{\ln(p)}$ is the expected life of the mosquito.

Vulnerability, also known as importation in risk assessment, refers to the likelihood of a system or community being exposed to hazards and their adverse effects, including both external exposures and internal processing capabilities. Furthermore, some researchers believe that population vulnerability should include social susceptibility, biological susceptibility, and the ability to respond.

8.3 Surveillance and Early Warning

8.3.1 *Malaria Surveillance*

Malaria monitoring includes investigations of infection sources (case detection), management of mobile populations, vector mosquito monitoring (population, number, biting rate, blood-sucking habits, vectorial capacity and sensitivity to insecticides), serological surveillance, epidemic investigation and handling, and monitoring of malaria parasite resistance, etc. In fact, both direct (parasitology, entomology, etc.) and indirect factors (natural, social factors) that constitute the occurrence, transmission, and recurrence of malaria are within the scope of surveillance. The World Health Organization recommends that malaria surveillance be the core intervention for malaria prevention and control. A robust surveillance system must insightfully gather information about care and case detection and demand comprehensive reporting from all health departments. As a core intervention measure, surveillance provides a foundation for implementing prevention and control measures in all transmission situations, with the aim of supporting the alleviation of the malaria burden, elimination of the disease, and prevention of its recurrence. However, in most countries at risk of vector-borne diseases, capacity for vector surveillance and control are both lacking. Additionally, many countries with more than one major vector-borne disease have specific prevention plans and measures for specific diseases, but these plans and strategies do not optimally promote coordination and may even compete for health resources. These countries need accurate and reliable surveillance systems to monitor the burden of malaria, the effects of interventions on malaria prevention and control, and their impacts across time and space (Mo and Yao 2006).

China, announced in 2021 by WHO as having successfully eliminated malaria, is the first country in the Western Pacific Region to announce the elimination of malaria after Australia (1981), Singapore (1982), and Brunei (1987). We can learn from China's experience and help countries struggling with malaria to formulate strategies for fighting against the disease. The "1-3-7" approach to malaria surveillance and response is a key measure adopted by China for malaria elimination, aimed at reporting malaria cases within 1 day following detection, conducting epidemiological investigation and categorization of patients within 3 days, and completing an investigation and response of the patient's surrounding environmental conditions within 7 days (Zhou 2022). The WHO has adopted this approach as part of its guidelines for directing global malaria control programs, particularly for countries or regions on the brink of eliminating malaria. As demonstrated by interactions between health authorities of China and Tanzania, China's sharing of its experience in malaria control has led to an 81% reduction in the burden of malaria in Tanzania (Liu et al. 2021).

After establishing a surveillance system, it is also necessary to periodically evaluate this system to identify key areas of surveillance that are lacking and to assess the completeness, timeliness, and accuracy of the data collected by the system. The results of the appraisal of the malaria surveillance system may be used to propose operational and priority suggestions for strengthening the system; these suggestions can also be used for mapping national and subnational strategic plans for malaria prevention and control. The World Health Organization and partners have developed a malaria surveillance system evaluation toolkit that is designed to assess the capacity of malaria surveillance systems or integrated disease surveillance systems in accurately capturing malaria cases and fatalities in all transmission environments. For more details and a step-by-step guide on how to perform the malaria surveillance evaluation, please refer to the implementation reference guide (https://www.who.int/publications/i/item/9789240055278) (Table 8.1).

8.3.2 Early Warning of Malaria

Carrying out malaria surveillance is the basis for early warning of malaria. Based on malaria surveillance data, such as the monitoring of malaria vector species and density, and discovery of imported cases, early warnings, swift responses, and timely handling of epidemics can prevent the outbreak of malaria. In countries and regions with well-established health monitoring networks, continuous disease surveillance, and complete historical data on malaria incidence, historical incidence data can be used for early warning of malaria. For example, a warning is triggered if the current number of cases exceeds 3/4 of the average monthly value over the past five years or the normal upper limit.

Also, based on the observation data on mosquito vector transmission potential, the vectorial capacity indicator, which can evaluate the potential for mosquito transmission, can not only evaluate the ability of different mosquito species to transmit malaria but also predict the trend of malaria occurrence by the vectorial capacity values of the main vectors in different seasons, thus completing the early warning.

In addition, early warning of malaria can be based on climate monitoring data. The transmission of malaria has seasonal characteristics, and the average seasonal climate can be predicted in time and space. Based on the seasonal climate forecast, seasonal rainfall levels that are higher than the average are predicted 1 to 6 months in advance, which can predict the risk of a malaria outbreak several months ahead.

Finally, the application of remote sensing and geographic information systems in malaria prediction and early warning is also worth learning from. By converting the map of malaria incidence rate into the map of malaria risk areas and combining disease factors (parasite infection, vector changes, length of incubation period, etc.) and environmental factors (temperature and rainfall, etc.), trend analysis, simulation and monitoring of the spread and diffusion of malaria can be performed from a spatiotemporal tracking and surveillance perspective.

Table 8.1 The malaria surveillance, monitoring, and evaluation toolkit

Function	Tools	Description
Define scope	Assessment Framework Tool	A set of key objectives, sub-objectives and indicators that can be used to quantify and qualify strengths and weaknesses in the surveillance system. This tool should be used as the starting point in an assessment to define the scope of the assessment and the approach
	Concept note and protocol	A template for the outline of a short concept note for refining the scope, methods, expected outputs and outcomes of an assessment, and a more detailed protocol outline required for comprehensive assessments
	Surveillance assessment planning tool	A budgeting template to assist countries in developing a costed plan to undertake a comprehensive assessment
Collect and analyse data	Desk Review Tool	A set of questions, tables, graphics and diagrams used to collect information and summarize what is known about malaria surveillance through document and data review, and optional interviews with surveillance programme staff and other relevant supporting partners
	Data quality assessment tools	Tools and guidance for collecting and analysing data to specifically assess data quality at national, regional, district and service delivery levels
	Question Bank	A library of questions that can be used to develop survey questionnaires for data collection at service delivery levels
	Analysis tools	A set of shell tables in Microsoft Excel that are used to summarize the results from the survey
Develop and prioritize recommendations	Technical brief and report outline	A report template for organizing, visualizing and interpreting results from the assessment. A technical brief is used to highlight a subset of priority results, whereas the complete report includes all assessment results

8.4 Prevention and Control Strategy and Measures

The "1-3-7" strategy, a distinctive malaria surveillance and response method initiated by China, has been a cornerstone in facilitating malaria elimination in the country. This systematic approach sets clear timelines: identifying and reporting malaria cases within a day of detection, performing an epidemiological investigation and classifying patients within a span of three days, and wrapping up an in-depth study and response concerning the patient's surrounding environmental conditions within a week. This timely and comprehensive strategy exemplifies the significance of prompt and coordinated action steps in combatting malaria. WHO, recognizing the effectiveness of the "1-3-7" approach, has incorporated this as a core part of its guidelines for directing global malaria control programs. This strategy takes on heightened importance in countries or regions teetering on the verge of malaria elimination, showcasing the significance of the "1-3-7" work model in shaping malaria control strategies on a global scale.

Malaria is primarily transmitted to humans by the bite of infected female mosquitoes, so malaria can be prevented by avoiding mosquito bites. In addition, medication can also be used to prevent malaria, and treatment can prevent the progression from mild to severe disease. Malaria prevention and control strategies include vector control, chemoprevention, prophylactic chemotherapy, immunization, and post-elimination control strategies, etc. (World Health Organization n.d.a).

8.4.1 Vector Control

Vector control is a critical component of the malaria control and elimination strategy because it is very effective in preventing infections and reducing disease transmission. Different species of mosquitoes have different capacities to transmit parasites, varying tolerances to vector control measures, and are affected by local environmental factors. Therefore, it is essential to implement vector control based on local epidemiological and entomological data. Currently, the World Health Organization recommends the deployment of one of the two widely used vector control interventions, namely, insecticide-treated nets (ITNs) and indoor residual spraying (IRS). National malaria plans need to ensure that all individuals at risk of malaria are protected through the provision, use, and timely replacement of ITNs, or regular use of IRS. Depending on the specific circumstances of a country, both ITNs and IRS can be deployed in different geographic areas; under specific conditions, other interventions can also be deployed, such as the common use of biological or chemical insecticides for larviciding in bodies of water.

In order to implement effective vector control measures, it is essential to integrate entomological surveillance, coverage monitoring, and impact assessment of vector control interventions into national surveillance systems. Countries should collect data across all environments, including areas without malaria but at risk of resumption of transmission.

However, the increasing physiological resistance of mosquitoes to insecticides is a significant threat. In many cases, malaria parasite transmission continues even when high coverage of ITNs or IRS has been achieved. Therefore, there is a need for further monitoring of local transmission dynamics, including resistance to insecticides and vector genomics, and for the introduction of new interventions to address resistance and fill existing intervention gaps.

8.4.2 *Chemoprevention*

Chemoprevention involves the periodic administration of anti-malarial drugs in doses lower than those used for treatment, but sufficient to prevent malaria. Travelers planning to visit malaria-endemic areas are advised to consult a doctor a few weeks before departure. Medical professionals will determine which chemoprevention drug is suitable for the destination country. In some cases, chemoprevention drugs must be started 2–3 weeks before departure. During a stay in a malaria-risk area, all prophylactic drugs should be taken on time and continued for 4 weeks after the last possible exposure because parasites may still emerge from the liver during this period. With improvements in malaria control and individuals not being exposed enough to malaria during their growth to develop naturally acquired immunity, considering the most appropriate use of malaria drugs to protect these individuals when visiting areas with malaria risk is becoming increasingly important.

8.4.3 *Prophylactic Chemotherapy*

Prophylactic chemotherapy involves the use of drugs, either alone or in combination, to prevent malaria infection and its consequences. It requires that a full course of anti-malarials be provided at designated points of time during the period of greatest malaria risk to vulnerable populations, whether or not the individuals treated are infected with malaria. Prophylactic chemotherapy includes perennial malaria chemoprevention (PMC), seasonal malaria chemoprevention (SMC), intermittent preventive treatment for pregnant women (IPTp) and school-aged children (IPTsc), post-discharge malaria chemoprevention (PDMC), and mass drug administrations (MDA). These safe and cost-effective strategies aim to complement ongoing malaria control activities, including vector control measures, prompt diagnosis of suspected malaria, and treatment of confirmed cases with anti-malarial drugs.

8.4.4 *Malaria Vaccine*

Malaria vaccines have the potential to be an important addition to a broad array of interventions in the future. Since October 2021, the World Health Organization has recommended the widespread use of the RTS,S/AS01 malaria vaccine among children living in areas of moderate to high Plasmodium falciparum transmission.

The vaccine has been shown to significantly reduce cases of malaria and fatal severe malaria in young children.

8.4.5 Post-Elimination Control Strategies

Some countries have achieved the World Health Organization's standard for malaria elimination, with routine surveillance and timely response forming the cornerstones of malaria control. Despite breaking local malaria transmission chains, countries that have eliminated malaria still face the risk of imported malaria. As the vectors that transmit malaria still exist in former endemic areas, there's a significant risk of local transmission sparked by imported cases in malaria elimination areas.

Malaria surveillance is not only one of the effective intervention measures for malaria elimination, but also an important task in the post-elimination phase. On December 31, 2020, China's National Health Commission and 13 other departments jointly issued the "Management Measures for Preventing the Re-transmission of Imported Malaria", clearly proposing a "timely detection, accurate prevention" strategy.

With a focus on surveillance work and core measures of surveillance and response, there has been an adjustment and optimization of work priorities on the basis of maintaining a surveillance and response system during the elimination phase. This includes continuing to maintain the malaria diagnosis and treatment capabilities of medical institutions and emphasizing timely detection and standardized treatment of imported malaria cases; enhancing the investigation and assessment of transmission risks of imported malaria cases, promptly handling and effectively blocking the re-transmission risks of epidemic points or populations at risk.

Eliminated malaria countries should focus on the following main content for malaria monitoring and response work: further improve the sensitivity of the surveillance system, improve the quality and efficiency of surveillance work; improve the malaria monitoring diagnostic laboratory network, improve the quality of monitoring data, and achieve the effect of maintaining malaria diagnostic capabilities with quality assurance; strengthen monitoring data analysis; further improve the joint prevention and control mechanism of multiple departments, strengthen the follow-up management of foreign workers returning to the country, including health education, monitoring and screening; and carry out vector surveillance, sensitivity monitoring of anti-malaria drugs, research and development and promotion of new monitoring technologies and information technologies.

8.5 Effect Evaluation

Malaria elimination certification is WHO's formal recognition of a country's malaria-free status. If a country can provide strict and credible evidence that the local mosquito-borne malaria transmission chain has been broken nationwide for at least three consecutive years, then WHO grants the certification. A country must also demonstrate the capacity to prevent the disease from re-emerging. The final decision to grant malaria-free certification is made by the WHO Director-General based on recommendations from an independent Malaria Elimination Certification Panel.

In 2015, WHO proposed *Global technical strategy for malaria 2016–2030* (GTS) to provide a comprehensive framework to guide countries in hastening the process of malaria elimination. The GTS set the goal of reducing global malaria incidence and mortality rates by at least 90% by 2030. Table 2.3 summarizes the phased goals for malaria elimination set by the GTS as well as the principles and strategic framework that should be adhered to during the elimination process (World Health Organization n.d.b) (Table 8.2).

For instance, in China, the history of malaria prevalence spans over three thousand years. During the 1940s and 1950s, there were 1829 malaria-endemic counties in China, with worst years seeing up to 30 million cases annually, seriously endangering the health and safety of the population. By 2010, China formulated the "China Malaria Elimination Action Plan (2010–2020)," which refined the work plan and proposed a case and epidemic-point-centered strategy of "clue tracing, clearing the source" and the "1-3-7" work norms. These norms specify that cases should be reported within 1 day of diagnosis, case review and epidemiological investigations should be completed within 3 days, and epidemic-point investigations and disposals should be done within 7 days.

In 2016, the last reported local case in China was in Yunnan. There have been no reports of primary infection cases since 2017. According to WHO standards, China achieved the goal of eliminating malaria in 2020, and in 2021, WHO sent experts to China for field assessments. They visited places like Yunnan, Hainan, Anhui, Hubei, and so forth. On June 30, 2021, the WHO officially announced that China had passed the certification for malaria elimination.

Table 8.2 Goals for *Global technical strategy for malaria 2016–2030*

Vision—A World Free of Malaria

Goals	Milestones		Targets
	2020	2025	2030
Reduce malaria mortality rates globally compared with 2015	At least 40%	At least 75%	At least 90%
Reduce malaria case incidence globally compared with 2015	At least 40%	At least 75%	At least 90%
Eliminate malaria from countries in which malaria was transmitted in 2015	At least 10 countries	At least 20 countries	At least 35 countries
Prevent re-establishment of malaria in all countries that are malaria-free	Re-establishment prevented	Re-establishment prevented	Re-establishment prevented

Principles

Country ownership and leadership, with involvement and meaningful participation of communities, are essential to accelerating progress through a multisectoral approach

All countries can accelerate efforts towards elimination through combinations of interventions tailored to local contexts

Improve impact through the use of data to stratify and tailor interventions to the local context

Equity in access to quality health services, especially for populations experiencing disadvantage, discrimination and exclusion, is essential

Innovation in interventions will enable countries to maximize their progression along the path to elimination

A resilient health system underpins the overall success of the malaria response

Strategic Framework——comprising three major pillars, with two supporting elements: (1) innovation and research, and (2) a strong enabling environment

Maximize impact of today's life-saving interventions
Pillar 1: Ensure access to malaria prevention, diagnosis and treatment as part of universal health coverage
Pillar 2: Accelerate efforts towards elimination and attainment of malaria-free status
Pillar 3: Transform malaria surveillance into a key intervention

Supporting element 1. Harnessing innovation and expanding research
Basic research to foster innovation and the development of new and improved interventions
Implementation research to optimize impact and cost-effectiveness of existing interventions
Action to facilitate rapid uptake of new interventions

Supporting element 2. Strengthening the enabling environment
Strong political and financial commitments
Multisectoral approaches, and cross-border and regional collaborations
Stewardship of entire heath system including the private sector, with strong regulatory support
Capacity development for both effective programme management and research

References

Chen TM, Zhang SS, Zhou SS (2017) Progress in research on risk assessment approach and parameters for malaria re-emergence. Chin J Parasitol Parasit Dis 35(5):489–494

Liu Q, Jing W, Kang L, et al. (2021, July 7) Trends of the global, regional and national incidence of malaria in 204 countries from 1990 to 2019 and implications for malaria prevention. J Travel Med 28(5):taab046. https://doi.org/10.1093/jtm/taab046.

Liu Q, Liu J (2023) A review on advances in global malaria epidemiology. Chin J Public Health 39(04):509–513

Mo SH (2006) Yao LN (2006) Monitoring, prediction, and early warning of malaria. Modern Practical Medicine 11:844–846

World Health Organization (n.d.a) World malaria report 2023. [EB/OL]. (2021–12–6)[2023–11–2] https://www.who.int/teams/global-malaria-programme/reports/world-malaria-report-2023

World Health Organization (n.d.b) Global technical strategy for malaria 2016–2030, 2021 update [EB/OL]. (2021–07–19)[2023–11–2] https://iris.who.int/handle/10665/342995

Zhou S (2022) Surveillance and response: The core intervention for malaria control during the post-elimination phase in China. Chin J Schisto Control 34(2):112–114. https://doi.org/10.16250/j.32.1374.2022077

Chapter 9
Practice of Risk Management on Viral Hepatitis

Viral hepatitis is a group of infectious diseases characterized by liver damage, caused by different hepatitis viruses. They are highly infectious and prevalent worldwide, with complex modes of transmission and high rates of infection. Depending on the pathogen, viral hepatitis primarily includes Hepatitis A, B, C, D, and E, caused by HAV, HBV, HCV, HDV, and HEV respectively.

Understanding the epidemiological patterns of viral hepatitis and taking effective prevention and control measures to curb its global prevalence and eliminate the public health threat it poses is one of the tasks to achieve the United Nations' sustainable development goals (SDGs). Viral hepatitis can be mainly divided into two types based on transmission modes. The first type is enterically transmitted viral hepatitis, primarily transmitted through food, water, and daily life contact. It has a certain seasonality, can cause outbreaks or epidemics, and infections are usually acute and self-limiting. This includes Hepatitis A and E.

The second type is non-enterically transmitted viral hepatitis, mainly transmitted through blood, mother-to-child (also known as vertical) transmission, and sexual contact. These types do not typically have seasonal patterns; infection results in acute viral hepatitis, which often turns into chronic hepatitis, and could lead to cirrhosis and hepatocellular carcinoma. This includes Hepatitis B, C, and D. Chronic B and C viral hepatitis in particular can lead to cirrhosis and liver cancer, accounting for 96% of all viral hepatitis mortality (World Health Organization n.d.a).

In 2016, the World Health Organization (WHO) approved the first global viral hepatitis strategy: *Elimination of Viral Hepatitis as a Public Health Threat by 2030*. It also released the *Global health sector strategy on viral hepatitis 2016–2021. Towards ending viral hepatitis*. In 2022, the WHO released the *Global health sector strategies on, respectively, HIV, viral hepatitis and sexually transmitted infections for the period 2022–2030* to hasten the realization of the ambitious goal of *Elimination of Viral Hepatitis as a Public Health Threat by 2030* (World Health Organization n.d.b; World Health Organization 2022). Globally, an estimated 325 million people are infected with Hepatitis B and/or C, for the majority of whom, testing and treatment

J. Liu, *Risk Management in Public Health*, Innovation in Risk Analysis,
https://doi.org/10.1007/978-981-97-6826-4_9

remain far from reach. As Hepatitis B and C cause chronic disease in hundreds of millions and are the most common causes of cirrhosis, cancer, and death from viral hepatitis, the global strategy WHO launched in 2022 focuses mainly on Hepatitis B and C. This chapter will thus mainly focus on the prevention and control of Hepatitis B as an example, aligning with the key areas of focus in the current global prevention and control strategy.

9.1 Disease Burden

HBV infection is a global epidemic. According to the World Health Organization, as of 2022, about 254 million people worldwide carry the Hepatitis B virus, with approximately 1.2 million new infections, and as high as 820,000 deaths associated with HBV. In terms of diagnosis, only 13.4% of chronic HBV infections were diagnosed globally, among which only 2.6% of the confirmed infections and 19.5% of total infections were receiving antiviral treatment. The African region faces a high rate of HBV infection, but only 18% of newborns have received the birth dose of Hepatitis B vaccine, underlining the urgency of expanding preventative measures.

On the other hand, the Western Pacific region has a higher coverage rate of Hepatitis B vaccination, but treatment coverage remains low. Moreover, some high-income countries, like the United States, are also facing the problem of increased HCV infection burden among drug users. China, India, Indonesia, Nigeria, Pakistan, Ethiopia, Bangladesh, Vietnam, the Philippines, and the Russian Federation collectively account for almost two-thirds of the global HBV and HCV infection burden. The progress of prevention and treatment efforts in these countries is crucial for global efforts to combat hepatitis.

A global Hepatitis B epidemiological survey conducted in China in 2014 showed that the prevalence of Hepatitis B surface antigen in people aged 1–29 was 2.94%, with the prevalence among children under 5 being 0.32%. According to estimates from the Polaris International Epidemiology Collaboration, the prevalence of Hepatitis B surface in the general population in China in 2016 was 6.1%, with 86 million cases of chronic HBV infection.

A systematic review and meta-analysis covering 231 million people in 2023 found that over nearly 50 years (1973–2021), the serum prevalence of Hepatitis B surface antigen in the general population declined from 9.6% (95% CI: 8.4–10.9%) between 1973 and 1984 to 3.0% (95% CI: 2.1–3.9%) in 2021. Among them, the decrease in the prevalence of Hepatitis B surface antigen in children under 5 years old was more pronounced than in adults, but the prevalence of Hepatitis B surface antigen in people aged 60 and over increased (Liu et al. 2023).

In general, the global burden of HBV infection is still heavy, and urgent measures are needed to expand effective interventions to save lives and prevent new infections, cancer cases, and deaths in future generations. At the same time, innovative methods must be employed to expand the prevention and treatment of Hepatitis B, targeting the specific conditions of different regions and countries.

9.2 Risk Assessment

9.2.1 Transmission Risk Assessment

HBV is primarily transmitted through mother-to-child transmission, blood, and sexual contact. In China, the predominant mode is mother-to-child, accounting for 40–50% of new infections, most of which occur perinatally. Studies have found that the levels of HBV DNA in a mother's body are closely related to the risk of a newborn contracting HBV. The higher the HBV DNA levels, the greater the risk of mother-to-child transmission, and the higher the likelihood of the newborn becoming infected with HBV.

In adults, the main transmission routes are through blood and sexual contact, such as the transfusion of unscreened and untested blood and blood products, invasive procedures that are not standard (such as surgery, injections, and dental treatments), irregular blood purification, and unprotected sexual conduct. In addition, HBV can also be transmitted through broken skin or mucous membranes, like occupational exposure, tattooing, ear piercing, shared razors, and tooth tools. Adults engaging in such unsafe behaviors are at a higher risk of infection.

HBV is not transmitted through respiratory or digestive routes. Therefore, daily work, study or life contact, such as working in the same office, shaking hands, hugging, living in the same dormitory, using common dining or toilet facilities, and other non-bloodborne exposures do not spread HBV (Chinese Society of Hepatology, Chinese Medical Association 2023).

9.2.2 Prognostic Risk Assessment

9.2.2.1 Chronification Risk Assessment

The natural history and prognosis of HBV infection mainly depend on the interaction between the virus and the host. Among the factors, the age of HBV infection is one of the most significant influencers for chronicity. Studies found that the risk of chronic infection after HBV infection in infants under 1 year old is 90%, while in adults the risk of chronification following HBV infection is less than 5%.

9.2.2.2 Liver Cirrhosis Risk Assessment

In patients with chronic Hepatitis B who do not undergo antiviral treatment, the annual incidence rate of cirrhosis is between 2 and 10%. The main risk factors include older age, being male, persistently elevated ALT levels, high viral load, co-infection with HCV, HDV or HIV, and accompanying adverse behavioral factors causing additional liver damage (such as alcoholism) or physical states (like obesity).

If cirrhosis decompensates, the five-year survival rate for patients is between 14 and 35%.

9.2.2.3 Liver Cancer Risk Assessment

Hepatocellular carcinoma (HCC) is the third leading cause of cancer-related deaths worldwide. Early identification of high-risk groups, early screening, diagnosis and treatment are one of the key measures to improve the survival rate of HCC. Studies show that in non-cirrhotic HBV infection, the annual incidence of HCC is between 0.2% and 1.0%. In cirrhotic HBV infected individuals, the annual incidence of HCC is between 3 and 6%. Among these, age > 40 years, male gender, cirrhosis, a family history of HCC, high level HBV replication, drinking, smoking, coexisting diabetes, obesity, and exposure to aflatoxin are all risk factors for the development of HCC.

The development of risk assessment and screening tools for HCC in chronic hepatitis patients is a global research hotspot. Risk prediction models are built using the risk factors for HCC and risk stratification is performed. For instance, some scholars built and validated the aMAP score based on a prospective global cohort of chronic hepatitis B patients. This score, constructed from five common test indicators including age, gender, platelets, albumin, and total bilirubin, gives a composite risk score range of 0–100 for HCC in chronic hepatitis patients. Patients can be divided into low-risk (0–50 points), medium-risk (50–60 points) and high-risk (60–100 points) groups based on their score. On this basis, some researchers have used multi-dimensional longitudinal data to optimize the construction of the aMAP-2 score and aMAP-2 Plus score, proposing that a sequential HCC screening strategy of aMAP—aMAP-2—aMAP-2 Plus is more feasible and cost-effective for guiding personalized HCC monitoring. For example, chronic liver disease patients can first use the aMAP score, the lowest cost and easiest tool, for risk assessment, avoiding overly frequent HCC screening in nearly 50% of people. Then the aMAP-2 and aMAP-2 Plus scores can sequentially be used in the remaining 50% of medium-to-high risk individuals defined by the aMAP score, to further screen for very high or ultra-high risk HCC patients. Finally, this strategy can spare 90% of low-risk HCC patients from frequent HCC screening, while guiding limited medical resources to focus on the remaining 10% of ultra-high risk HCC individuals, providing a combined screening strategy for high-risk HCC populations in chronic liver disease patients (Fan et al. 2023).

9.3 Surveillance and Early Warning

Many countries have not the epidemiologic information needed to plan, implement, monitor, evaluate and update national viral hepatitis prevention and control strategies. Technical aspects related to viral hepatitis surveillance are considered complex and there is little available guidance. In the absence of a reliable evidence base, viral hepatitis remains a silent epidemic. However, tools exist to optimize surveillance and generate information that can effectively guide prevention, control and treatment policies. In 2010 and 2014, World Health Assembly resolutions called for enhanced surveillance of viral hepatitis (World Health Assembly 2010). Therefore, WHO has developed these technical considerations to assist and guide Member States in implementing and/or optimizing viral hepatitis surveillance (Table 9.1) (World Health Organization 2016).

The purposes of viral hepatitis surveillance include the following:

1) Detect outbreaks, monitor trends in incidence and identify risk factors for new, incident infections. This is achieved through surveillance for acute hepatitis. Surveillance for acute hepatitis may be done in two ways. A basic approach is to do surveillance for unspecified acute hepatitis (referred to as "syndromic surveillance") defined on the basis of clinical signs and symptoms. Surveillance for unspecified acute hepatitis in all health-care facilities allows for the detection and investigation of outbreaks. If resources allow, surveillance with quality in vitro diagnosis will help to detect clusters and describe trends. If combined with collection of epidemiological information, this type of surveillance can also identify risk factors for new infections. Surveillance that combines in vitro diagnosis and collection of epidemiological information is resource intensive. Hence, implementation in selected geographical areas and/or health-care facilities (referred to as "sentinel sites") is often a preferred option, particularly in resource-limited settings.

   Surveillance for acute hepatitis is conducted to some extent in many countries but may require technical improvement and clarification of objectives. Use of standardized case definitions based on the clinical presentation and on the presence of biomarkers allows cases of acute hepatitis to be separated from cases of chronic infection.
2) Estimate the prevalence of chronic infections and monitor trends in sentinel groups. This is done through biomarker surveys that estimate the proportion of the population that is chronically infected in order to plan for testing, management and care. These surveys are ideally integrated with surveys conducted for other purposes (e.g. HIV surveys) and may be repeated over time. Reporting of chronic HBV and HCV infections in health-care facilities can also be used to estimate the number of cases identified and managed in health-care services. This does not constitute a reliable method of estimating burden, as many chronically infected persons never seek care. Repeated visits to health-care facilities may lead to duplicate reporting that needs to be eliminated.
3) Estimate the burden of disease associated with chronic infections, including cirrhosis, liver failure and hepatocellular carcinoma, and their risk of death. This is achieved through the use of cancer registries, death certification, and estimates of the prevalence of HBV and HCV infection among cases of cirrhosis and hepatocellular carcinoma (HCC). This may be implemented in selected sentinel tertiary reference centers. Multiplying the estimated number of deaths

Table 9.1 Viral hepatitis surveillance: Technical approaches that may be used to reach specific objectives for acute hepatitis, chronic infections and sequelae

Technical approaches:	If the objective of hepatitis surveillance is to:				
	Detect outbreaks	Describe trends in type-specific acute hepatitis and identify risk factors	Estimate the proportion of chronically infected persons who have been identified	Estimate the burden of chronic infections Model incidence trends	Estimate the incidence of HCC and cirrhosis
Preferred surveillance methods:	Syndromic surveillance in the general population Event-based surveillance[a]	Enhanced case reporting (with in vitro diagnosis and collection of information on risk factors), countrywide or in sentinel sites[b]	Case reporting from laboratories or health-care facilities	Regular surveys	Combination of data from: 1. Cancer registries 2. Death certificates 3. Testing of cirrhosis and HCC patients for HBV and HCV infection
Population under surveillance:	Persons presenting with acute hepatitis in health-care facilities (discrete onset of symptoms)		Persons without acute symptoms tested in health-care facilities/ laboratories	Persons without acute symptoms tested during population surveys	Persons diagnosed with cirrhosis and HCC
Condition to look for:	Unspecified acute hepatitis	Type-specific acute hepatitis	Biomarker evidence of past or present infection Chronic infection, irrespective of symptoms		Cases of HCC or cirrhosis with chronic HBV or HCV infection
Analysis and reporting will characterize:	Acute hepatitis that reflects new infections		Burden of chronic, prevalent infections		Burden of sequelae

HBV: hepatitis B virus, HCC: hepatocellular carcinoma, HCV: hepatitis C virus
[a]In vitro diagnosis needs to be organized on a sample of cases when an outbreak is reported
[b]High-quality data (i.e. reliable in vitro diagnosis, good information on risk factors) from a smaller number of tertiary centres is preferable and more efficient than poor-quality data from many sites

from cirrhosis, HCC and liver failure by the fractions of disease attributable to HBV and HCV can estimate this burden.

The principles of surveillance for different hepatitis viruses are the same. However, WHO has proposed standardized case definitions for viral hepatitis A, B, C and E

(Tables 9.2 and 9.3) (World Health Organization 2016). These technical considerations do not provide specific guidance or definitions for hepatitis D surveillance. However, the general principles described in these technical considerations will apply to the surveillance of hepatitis D.

Table 9.2 WHO surveillance case definitions for acute viral hepatitis[a]

Level of case definition	Acute hepatitis			
Presumptive case: Clinical criteria	Discrete onset of an acute illness with signs/symptoms of (i) acute infectious illness (e.g. fever, malaise, fatigue) and (ii) liver damage (e.g. anorexia, nausea, jaundice, dark urine, right upper quadrant tenderness, AND/OR raised alanine aminotransferase (ALT) levels more than ten times the upper limit of normal)[b]			
Confirmed case: Clinical criteria AND biomarker or epidemiological criteria	Hepatitis A	Acute hepatitis E	Acute hepatitis B	Acute hepatitis C
	IgM anti-HAV + ve OR Epidemiological link with a confirmed case[c]	IgM anti-HEV + ve OR Epidemiological link with a confirmed case[d]	IgM anti-HBc + ve[e,f]	HCV RNA + ve and anti-HCV −ve OR
				Seroconversion to anti-HCV[g] OR
				Anti-HCV + ve AND IgM anti-HBc −ve AND Anti-HAV IgM −ve AND Anti-HEV IgM -ve

Ag: antigen, anti-HAV: antibody against hepatitis A virus, anti-HBc: antibody against hepatitis B core antigen, anti-HCV: antibody against hepatitis C virus, anti-HEV: antibody against hepatitis E virus, Ig: immunoglobulin, RNA: ribonucleic acid

[a]These case definitions are for the purpose of reporting and surveillance and may differ from criteria to be used for the management of patients

[b]Ten times the upper limit of normal (400 IU/L) is the threshold used by the State and Territorial Epidemiologists. Countries may also select lower thresholds that could be more sensitive or higher thresholds that could be more specific

[c]Contact with a confirmed case-patient during the referent exposure period or context of an etiologically confirmed outbreak

[d]Context of an etiologically confirmed outbreak

[e]Hepatitis test panels usually include HBsAg with anti-HBc IgM test. The positive predictive value of anti-HBc IgM is higher if HBsAg is positive

[f]A specific test and/or threshold is needed to exclude transient presence of IgM during flares among patients with chronic HBV infection

[g]Among patients tested regularly at short time intervals, seroconversion to anti-HCV suggests a recent HCV infection, which may take place in the absence of clinical, acute hepatitis. Seroconversion to anti-HCV should be followed by a reflex RNA test (when available)

Table 9.3 WHO surveillance case definitions for chronic viral hepatitis

<table>
<tr><th colspan="2"></th><th>Chronic HBV infection</th><th colspan="2">Hepatitis C</th></tr>
<tr><td rowspan="3">Only confirmed cases that all require clinical and biomarker criteria</td><td>Clinical criteria</td><td colspan="3">Person not meeting the case definition for acute hepatitis (e.g. person tested in the context of the evaluation of a chronic liver disease, a check-up or a survey)</td></tr>
<tr><td rowspan="2">Biomarker criteria</td><td rowspan="2">HBsAg + ve[a]</td><td>Serological evidence of past or present infection</td><td>Chronic HCV infection</td></tr>
<tr><td>Anti-HCV + ve</td><td>HCV RNA + ve
OR
HCV Ag + ve</td></tr>
</table>

Ag: antigen, anti-HCV: antibody against hepatitis C virus, HBsAg: hepatitis B surface antigen, HBV: hepatitis B virus, HCV: hepatitis C virus, RNA: ribonucleic acid

[a]Most testing strategies would also test for total anti-HBc. The combination of total anti-HBc and HBsAg is more specific of chronic HBV infection than HBsAg alone

9.4 Prevention and Control Strategy and Measures

In order to better achieve the United Nations Sustainable Development Goals (SDGs) to "combat hepatitis", the WHO released the Global health sector strategy on viral hepatitis 2016–2021 in 2016, which sets the ambitious goal of "eliminating viral hepatitis as a public health threat by 2030", which aims to reduce new hepatitis infections by 90% and deaths by 65% between 2016 and 2030 (compared to 2015). Its specific core objectives are to reduce the hepatitis B surface antigen positivity rate from 1.3% in 2015 to 0.1% in 2030 among children under 5 years of age globally, and to reduce the number of HBV-related deaths from 887 thousand in 2015 to 310 thousand in 2030 (World Health Organization 2016).

In order to accelerate the global process of the elimination strategy, the WHO released the Global health sector strategies on, respectively, HIV, viral hepatitis and sexually transmitted infections for the period 2022–2030 in 2022 to provide guidance for the health sector to implement responses that are strategically focused in nature in order to achieve elimination goals by 2030. Based on the theory of change (Fig. 9.1), the strategy's vision, goals, strategic directions and targets are shown in Table 9.4 (World Health Organization 2022).

For viral hepatitis, Strategic Direction One is to provide high quality, evidence-based, person-centered services. This refers to the use of evidence-based guidance and innovations in service delivery to accelerate access to and utilization of a range of high-quality essential and other relevant health services for viral hepatitis to meet the specific needs of people in a range of populations and settings, ensuring that no one is left behind. Strategic Direction Two is to optimize systems, sectors and partnerships for impact. It refers to a systems-focused approach that promotes synergies with primary health care, health governance, financing, human resources, commodities

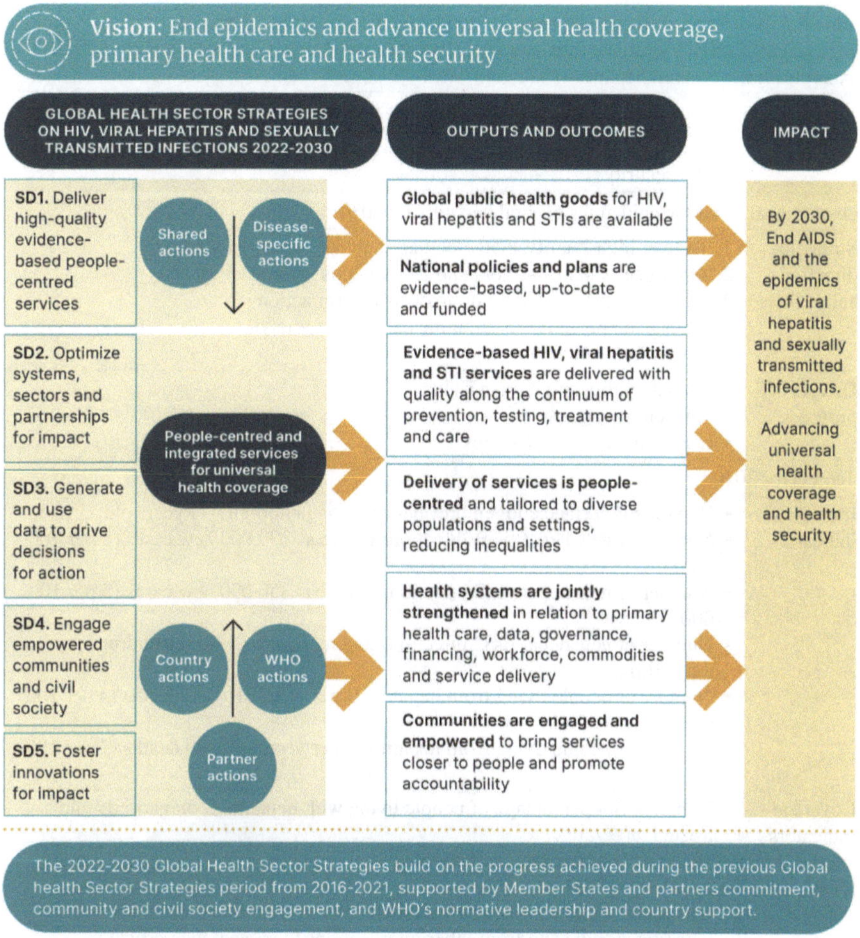

Fig. 9.1 Theory of change

and service delivery, while fostering multisectoral responses to the social and structural determinants of health. Coordination and collaboration with partners, including funders, academic and research institutions, professional groups and private sector entities, is undertaken to maximize impact. Strategic Direction Three is the generation and use of data to drive operational decision-making. It refers to the collection, analysis and use of evidence and data, disaggregated by sex, age and other relevant demographic characteristics, to monitor and evaluate progress, guide action, innovation and research and development, and promote greater data transparency and accountability. Strategic Direction Four is to engage empowered communities and civil society. By engaging communities and civil society, including key and affected populations, and supporting their self-empowerment, they play a key role in advocacy, service delivery and decision-making, including ensuring that services are culturally

Table 9.4 Vision, overall goal, strategic direction and targets of the Global health sector strategies on, respectively, HIV, viral hepatitis and sexually transmitted infections for the period 2022–2030 (excerpts related to viral hepatitis)

Vision, overall goal, strategic direction and drivers of progress	
Vision	End epidemics and advance universal health coverage, primary health care and health security
Overall goal	End the epidemics of viral hepatitis by 2030
Strategic directions and actions	1. Deliver high-quality, evidence-based, people-centered services 2. Optimize systems, sectors and partnerships for impact 3. Generate and use data to drive decisions for action 4. Engage empowered communities and civil society 5. Foster innovations for impact
Drivers of progress	• Gender, equity and human rights • Financing • Leadership and partnerships
Targets for 2030	
Impact indicators	• Hepatitis B surface antigen prevalence among children 0–4 years old: 0.1%[a] • Number of new hepatitis B infections per year: 170 000 new cases (2 per 100 000) • Number of new hepatitis C infections per year: 350 000 new cases (5 per 100 000) • Number of new hepatitis C infections among persons who inject drugs per year: 2 per 100 • Number of people dying from hepatitis B per year: 310 000 deaths (4 per 100 000) • Number of people dying from hepatitis C per year: 140 000 deaths (2 per 100 000)
Coverage indicators	• Hepatitis B—percentage of people living with hepatitis B diagnosed / and treated: 90%/80% • Hepatitis C—percentage of people living with hepatitis C diagnosed / and cured: 90%/80% • Percentage of newborns who have benefitted from a timely birth dose of hepatitis vaccine and from other interventions to prevent the vertical (mother-to-child) transmission of hepatitis B virus: 90%[b] • Hepatitis B vaccine coverage among children (third dose): 90% • Number of needles and syringes distributed per person who injects drugs: 300[c] • Blood safety—proportion of blood units screened for bloodborne diseases:100% • Safe injections—proportion of safe health-care injections: 100%

[a]Please note that the targets in this table are global targets and should be adapted by Member States according to the national context when setting country targets. For example, in some countries a target for the prevalence of hepatitis B surface antigen among children younger than five years old may be less than 0.1% or 0.2%, although the overall global target is 0.1%

[b]In addition, the proportion of infants younger than 12 months of age who received the third dose of hepatitis B vaccine should also be measured as well as other indicators for preventing vertical transmission such as maternal testing and prophylaxis

[c]As part of a comprehensive harm reduction strategy and in line with national priorities

appropriate and responsive to the needs of the community, while addressing stigmatization and discrimination and removing social and structural barriers. Strategic direction five is to promote innovation for impact. It refers to working with partners to assist in the development and implementation of national, regional and global research and innovation agendas, prioritizing the development of new technologies, service delivery models and health system practices and overcoming key barriers to progress in the fight against viral hepatitis (World Health Organization 2022).

9.5 Effect Evaluation

HBV infection is one of the major public health issues worldwide, with China bearing a high burden of infection. China is therefore a key contributor to the elimination of public health threats caused by viral hepatitis. In the past few decades, China has made significant progress in the prevention and management of hepatitis B. This section uses the effectiveness of hepatitis B prevention and control in China as a case study for effectiveness evaluation.

Over the past 40 years, China has implemented comprehensive measures for the prevention and control of HBV, primarily focusing on immunization and treatment. The government has introduced a series of laws, policies, and technical guidelines, ensuring the implementation of comprehensive prevention and control for HBV from aspects of systems, funding, technology, etc., achieving significant progress (Fig. 9.2) (Liu and Liu 2019).

Overall, thanks to the implementation of China's comprehensive strategy and measures for hepatitis B prevention and control over the past forty years, new infections of hepatitis B in China have decreased significantly. The positive rate of hepatitis B surface antigen in the general population in China has decreased from 9.75% in 1992 and 7.18% in 2006 to currently 6%. Multiple studies have confirmed that China has transitioned from a high prevalence country for hepatitis B to a medium prevalence country. Currently, the positive rate for hepatitis B surface antigen in children under 5 years has decreased from 9.9% in 1992 to 0.3% in 2014, approaching the global target of 0.1% by 2030.

Mother-to-child transmission is a crucial route of transmission for hepatitis B virus in China. The standard management of HBV-infected pregnant women and their newborns can effectively prevent HBV mother-to-child transmission.

Recently, data from a national observational study on HBV infection among pregnant women in China for the first time showed that the prevalence rate of HBV infection among pregnant women in China decreased continuously from 2015 to 2020. The study's data came from the Chinese National Project for the Prevention of AIDS, Syphilis, and Hepatitis B Mother-to-child Transmission. In 2015–2020, a total of 90.87 million pregnant women from 2853 counties in mainland China underwent HBV detection, with approximately 5.6 million being detected with HBV infection (defined as positive for hepatitis B surface antigen).

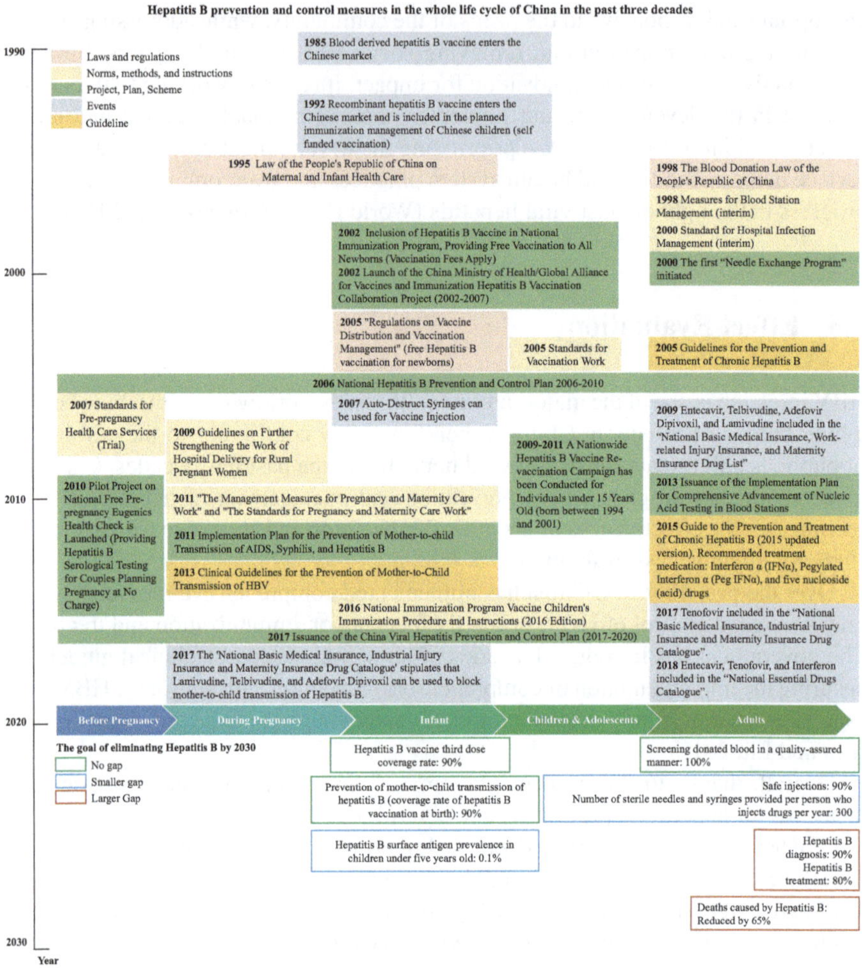

Fig. 9.2 Comprehensive measures and gap with the global 2030 hepatitis elimination goal in China

Regarding hepatitis B related deaths, according to global health monitoring data, the estimated death rate related to hepatitis B in China in 2016 was about 23/100,000 people, accounting for 38.6% of global deaths related to hepatitis B, and the diagnostics coverage and treatment rate for HBV infection were only 19% (global 2015 baseline: < 5%, 2030 target: 90%) and < 10–11% (global 2015 baseline: < 1%, 2030 target: 80%), respectively. Compared to the substantial achievements made in reducing new infections, the progress towards the goal of reducing hepatitis B-related deaths has been slower in China.

Future challenges lie mainly in reducing the burden of hepatitis B-related deaths, which is a common challenge faced globally. How to timely achieve the goal of eliminating the threat to public health posed by hepatitis B by 2030, as proposed by WHO, is a common global focus.

From the perspective of whole life cycle management, it is recommended to integrate existing public health and medical services projects, establish a comprehensive prevention and control system covering the whole life cycle of HBV infection prevention, screening, diagnosis, treatment, and rehabilitation. For example, by integrating the National Pre-pregnancy Eugenics Check-up Project and the National Project for the Prevention of AIDS, Syphilis and Hepatitis B Mother-to-child Transmission, a unique opportunity and management platform can be provided to better achieve the goal of eliminating hepatitis B by 2030. Health workers can utilize this platform to identify pregnant women and high-risk family members infected with HBV at an early stage of the disease, implement HBV prevention and control for a whole life cycle management at the unit of positive families, covering prevention and disease management of HBV infection in all life stages, reducing mortality and facilitating China's early achievement of the elimination of the public health threat posed by hepatitis B as targeted by the WHO.

References

Chinese Society of Hepatology, Chinese Medical Association (2023) Chinese Society of Infectious Diseases, Chinese Medical Association. Guidelines for the prevention and treatment of chronic hepatitis B (version 2022). J Prac Hepatol 41(1):3–28

Fan R, Chen L, Zhao S et al (2023) Novel, high accuracy models for hepatocellular carcinoma prediction based on longitudinal data and cell-free DNA signatures. J Hepatol 79(4):933–944. https://doi.org/10.1016/j.jhep.2023.05.0

Liu J, Liu M (2019) Progress and challenges in achieving the WHO goal on 'Elimination of Hepatitis B by 2030' in China. Chin J Epidemiol 40(6):605–609

Liu Z, Lin C, Mao X et al (2023) October 5) Changing prevalence of chronic hepatitis B virus infection in China between 1973 and 2021: a systematic literature review and meta-analysis of 3740 studies and 231 million people. Gut 72(12):2354–2363. https://doi.org/10.1136/gutjnl-2023-330691

World Health Assembly (2010) Viral hepatitis. https://iris.who.int/handle/10665/3092 (accessed 2 May 2024)

World Health Organization (2016) Technical considerations and case definitions to improve surveillance for viral hepatitis. https://www.who.int/publications/i/item/technical-considerations-and-case-definitions-to-improve-surveillance-for-viral-hepatitis-report (accessed 2 May 2024)

World Health Organization (2022) Global health sector strategies on, respectively, HIV, viral hepatitis and sexually transmitted infections for the period 2022–2030.Geneva: World Health Organization

World Health Organization (n.d.a) Global hepatitis report 2024. https://www.who.int/publications/i/item/9789240091672

World Health Organization (n.d.b) Global health sector strategy on viral hepatitis 2016–2021. Towards ending viral hepatitis. https://www.who.int/publications/i/item/WHO-HIV-2016.06 (accessed 2 May 2024)